Unlocked

Unlocked

TRANSFORM YOUR BARRIERS INTO
STRENGTHS AND BECOME THE LEADER
YOU WANT TO BE

REARN NORMAN

Psychologist and Leadership Coach

Contents

Acknowledgement of Country

I respectfully acknowledge the Wurundjeri People of the Kulin Nation, who are the Traditional Owners of the land on which this book was written.

I pay respect to their Elders, past, present and emerging.

Why this Book?

After nearly 20 years of practice working with hundreds of leaders as a psychologist and leadership coach, I found myself at a personal tipping point. I knew I was as committed as ever to my work. I was also becoming increasingly aware of a consistent set of patterns I was observing in leaders. These patterns had almost nothing to do with the technical part of how these leaders were operating; rather, they had everything to do with the way they were thinking and their behaviour.

As I went about helping my clients address these patterns and transform their working lives, I couldn't help but wonder about the many leaders outside my circle who may be looking for guidance. Writing a book like this was something I wanted to do, but I held back because it was also a very daunting prospect (more on that later!). In the end, I was driven by something much greater than fear or discomfort. Specifically, the desire to help you (and hopefully many other leaders) become more deeply aware of how you operate as a leader now, and to give you the tools and insights to make positive changes in line with the leader you want to be.

I believe we all need to access our full leadership potential to successfully navigate the world we live in. I've seen firsthand what happens when leaders become stuck. Not only does it affect them personally, but it also impacts those around them. When I've worked with leaders to grow their understanding of who they are and how they operate, using the principles in this book, I've seen them go on to thrive in ways they could not have imagined.

The first and key message of this book is that your team, organisation and the people around you need your leadership. They need you to step into your role as a leader; they need you to overcome any of the internal barriers we'll explore in this book that are getting in your way. The good news is that this act of leadership is not just on your shoulders. The people around you can help you to reach your full potential.

This book is not a technical manual, a book on 'how to do leadership' or a to-do list of actions claiming to make you a brilliant leader. It is a guide to help you go within, to start the critical work of growing your self-awareness, so you can also lead others brilliantly. This book will help you reflect on the leader you want to be. It will provide you with practical, evidence-based strategies to overcome the most common internal barriers that leaders experience.

You already have everything within you to be a great leader, the type of leader the world needs right now. It's just a matter of unlocking your potential.

Let's get started.

—

CHAPTER ONE

The World Needs Your Leadership

Whether you are in a leadership role at this moment or you're about to move into one, your potential is firstly determined by how you see yourself. When you have the self-awareness and tools needed to unlock your potential, you become an essential part of the world's collective leadership. The world has never needed great leaders more than it does right now. We're all looking for a path through some of the really big challenges we collectively face, and we need leaders to help show us the way.

This chapter is my call to action to all leaders and potential leaders; to those with the ability, commitment and heart to take on a leadership role (of any kind). Whether it's leading in the workplace, the community or your personal life, your leadership is needed. It's not about setting lofty or unrealistic expectations beyond what you seek or are capable of achieving; it's about recognising the value you can uniquely contribute, and acting on that for the greater good.

Your unique leadership is needed to help make decisions, support others, create positive change and provide guidance towards future – and better – outcomes. An important first step to unlocking your potential is recognising that you already hold a number of leadership roles and you've done so for some time. In appreciating this, you will start to see the potential you have to make a difference as a leader in many different ways.

Technology can do lots of amazing things, but it can't do the work of leadership. Emotionally connecting with others, empathising with them, developing a vision, communicating a message, creativity, imagination and generating possibilities can only come from human beings. Your perspective is a unique source of all of that. No one can create those outcomes in the same way you can.

Consider the roles you play in all parts of your life – at work, in the community, with friends and family and in your wider social networks. Do you try to create positive change? Do you work with others to achieve outcomes? Think about the projects that you are or have been involved in, the skills and knowledge you pass on to others. Consider the outcomes you are trying to achieve and your ability to develop a vision or hold a point of view on how things could be, working with others to achieve those outcomes. My message here is to start to see yourself as a leader in the broadest sense possible, because this is where your biggest potential for impact lies.

WHAT LEADERSHIP IS ... AND IS NOT

Leadership is ultimately about behaviour and ways of thinking. It's not a role that you are appointed to or a badge that someone pins to your chest. Think of it this way: there are so many appointed 'leaders' who are pretty terrible human beings and don't care too much about the impact they have on others. At the same time, there's an incredible amount of people that I've met (and I'm sure you have too) who are truly great at achieving outcomes with other people. They have colleagues and team members who would do anything for them, largely because of the person they are and how they interact with others.

By necessity, good leadership also lacks ego. I like to think that leadership is about acting for the collective, and being able to observe what's happening as the collective acts around you. Great leaders try to take themselves out of the equation. They don't think of themselves as a sole central figure trying to control all the outcomes and solve all the problems. These leaders place great levels of trust in those around them. When they do, the benefits always follow.

Leadership is about acting for the collective, and being able to observe what's happening as the collective acts around you.

Not everyone must or will choose to take up the role of leader. That is completely okay, so long as that choice is not influenced adversely by fear, assumptions about your own potential, or others' negative and critical voices. And if you are here reading this book, I'm assuming you are already motivated to lead! You alone should determine how you see your own identity, including how you see yourself as a leader.

THE COMPLEXITY GAP

In every conversation I have with leaders across all walks of life, the story I hear is consistent – the role of leadership is both deeply rewarding and challenging. In particular, the pace of change and increasing complexity we face means you need to continuously grow as a leader. By change and complexity, I'm talking about technological and sociocultural change – how we live our lives, how we use technology, how we engage with each other and how we experience the world. In many ways, the current pace of change is greater than the ability our brains and bodies have to adapt. As a society and as human beings, we are struggling to keep up. We can't rely on the practices of old or the ways of thinking we've always held. As the world changes around us, we must too – especially if we seek to lead the way.

As I write this book in early 2022, we are still recovering from more than two years of the global COVID-19 pandemic. There is horrific destruction in Ukraine at the hands of Russian invaders. We're seeing devastating images of one-in-1000-year floods in Queensland and New South Wales – the direct result of the climate disaster we all face. Of course, I'm not saying that any one person is charged with fixing these huge, complex issues, but I argue that all of these events could be considered a result of deficits in leadership. They are all examples of how we need more effective leadership in the world.

Some may argue: 'If we're being outpaced by complexity, what will it matter if I change or not? Even if we're changing and growing, won't we still be behind?' I feel this argument deeply and have wondered the same. But as leaders we *can* make a difference. We can show others the way forward by understanding ourselves better, taking the opportunity to learn and develop, and building our capacity to lead through challenging times. If we do that, we can better access the collective potential of leaders to help face these complex challenges together.

LEADERSHIP EXISTS IN THE INTERACTION BETWEEN PEOPLE

Leadership is at its core what psychologists describe as dyadic – it exists only as an interaction between (at least two) people. You cannot be a leader in isolation of everyone and everything else; it is a deeply human experience. You must be perceived as a leader by others and achieve outcomes through others in order to 'qualify' as a leader. And because leadership exists through the relationships you have with others, who you are as a person is inextricably linked with how you lead. Who you are includes how you think, your values and beliefs, your background and experience, your personality, your assumptions about the world, and your behaviours.

Knowing this about leadership means you cannot escape from yourself as you take up your role as a leader. You are more effective as a leader when you have a deep understanding of who you are and how you bring those qualities directly and authentically to how you lead. It's also what makes your leadership unique.

My study and practice in organisational psychology over the last 20 years has shown me that the study of leadership and management is grounded in the science of human behaviour – understanding what 'makes us tick'. Those fields tell us that without human interaction, there is no leadership. Think about the interactions you have had with leaders in your own life, whether those interactions were fantastic, good, neutral or terrible. What made them so? Was it the leader's technical ability and knowledge? Was it what they achieved in their role? Or was it more related to who they were as a person and how they interacted with you? When I ask people these questions, most refer to the latter. Echoing a favourite Maya Angelou quote:

'I've learned that people will forget what you said, people will forget what you did, but people will never forget how you made them feel.'

Reflecting on how much of our leadership is shaped by who we are as a person might be pretty confronting. You might be thinking, 'But I've spent a large chunk of my work life with my "work mask" on. Showing who I truly and fully am as a person would be too risky.' I distinctly remember feeling like this, especially early on in my career. As a young female working in the corporate world, I would be hyper-conscious of how I dressed and the mannerisms I used – especially around older, male clients. I would go out of my way to appear way more 'serious' than my family or friends would ever recognise me to be, in an attempt to build credibility. It was exhausting!

To be anything other than yourself as a leader comes at too great a cost. To live and work while keeping parts of who you are in separate realms takes an inordinate amount of energy. You're likely to get caught out at some stage. You will inadvertently drop the mask. Furthermore, wearing a mask is dishonouring all that is really great and unique about you as a person. It's not an easy task to start bringing more of who you are to how you lead, but in this book I'll guide you on how to do that safely.

To what extent do the people in your work life know who you truly are as a person? I'm not talking about knowing every intimate detail about your life! But if they were to describe you, would they describe the person that you know yourself to be, and that your family and friends know you to be? A first step might be to talk about this with a trusted friend or colleague. Are there any ways in which you are keeping your true self out of the way you lead? What is the impact or cost of that to you, to the people around you, and to the work that you're doing?

You might hold concerns about the risk of bringing more of who you are into how you lead. It might invoke feelings of vulnerability. That's perfectly understandable. You don't have to overcome this challenge at a moment's notice. For now, just become aware of how much of your true self is showing or hiding in how you lead.

WHEN WOMEN LEAD, ORGANISATIONS AND SOCIETY BENEFIT

This chapter is also a call to unlock the leadership potential of more women. We continue to see a gender imbalance in many countries, industries and facets of society, particularly at senior leadership levels in organisations. This imbalance comes at great cost to those organisations and workplaces, as well as to women themselves who suffer from bias and inequality of opportunity. The world needs leaders everywhere to unlock their potential, but we especially need more women to do this. If you are someone who identifies as a woman, this is a particular call to action for you to unlock your potential – fully acknowledging the systemic challenges that many women face in their work lives. If you are someone who does not identify as a woman, being aware of the gender imbalance is key as you consider the opportunity for you to advocate for women in leadership, and demonstrate inclusive leadership yourself.

I've read dozens of studies over the years that provide evidence of the benefits to organisations and society when women lead. The Australian government's Workplace Gender Equality Agency (WGEA) aims to promote and improve gender equality in Australian workplaces. In its 2020 research paper it stated:

> *More women in key decision-making positions delivers better company performance, greater productivity and greater profitability. Increasing the representation of women across each of the key leadership roles in an organisation added a market value of between AU$52 million and AU$70 million per year for an average-sized organisation.*

Enough said!

There are many external barriers (such as bias, discrimination and systemic issues) that prevent or slow the progress of women in leadership compared to men. I fully acknowledge those external barriers exist, and have experienced some of them directly myself. I haven't written this book to arm you with silver bullets for destroying those barriers. What I have focused on is what I believe to be 'step one' – control the controllables. My aim is to support you to understand and overcome any internal barriers you experience, so you are in the best position possible to navigate those external barriers as and when you face them.

Ultimately, I'm not intending to generalise. We are all individuals and those individual differences are what make us human. I'm also not saying that women are broken and need 'fixing'! I am saying that we need more women to lead with their full potential. The tools and ideas I share in this book will hopefully be of service in helping more women achieve that.

We all recognise and acknowledge that the external barriers we've talked about will not go away anytime soon. Culture, society and other people can at times negatively reinforce messages about your potential and your place in leadership. As a result, you might forget the messages I'm sharing here that your leadership is needed, in which case I encourage you to come back to this book as you need to.

STEPPING INTO YOUR LEADERSHIP

This book is designed to give you space to think about your potential, what you want to achieve and the impact you want to have as a leader. I will encourage and guide you to invoke the curiosity needed to learn how to think and behave in slightly different but powerful ways, while staying true to who you are at your core. As an individual, you have within you the potential to make a valuable and significant difference through your leadership – whether that is at work, in the community or in your personal life. While the world continues to change and become more complex, you can lead from a place of knowing who you are as a person while continuing to develop and grow.

This chapter may feel like a big call to action – and it is. But the world faces many challenges and opportunities right now, and leadership is the resource everyone is looking for to help find their way through. We need as many capable people as possible stepping up as leaders, and you are one. I encourage you to start noticing all the ways and opportunities you have to lead already. And to consider, with curiosity and openness, the many ways you could lead in the future.

Now that you have embraced the idea that your leadership is needed in the world, it's time to focus on the factors that are always within your control: the way you think, behave and make sense of the world around you. It's time to look within.

CHAPTER TWO

—

Starting from Within

At any stage of career, your inner world (how you think, feel and make sense of situations) can be the single biggest factor that influences your effectiveness as a leader. I've met many incredible people – from emerging through to experienced leaders – who are clever, hardworking and seemingly have it all together, only to discover through speaking with them how much their inner world affects them every day.

It's not just the inner world we have to contend with as leaders, obviously. There will always be loads of challenges and situations we must work through. But you will be better armed to deal with these external challenges when you focus on what must be dealt with first – the barriers within. I see so many leaders trying to push through, working so hard but unconsciously experiencing these barriers at the same time. The image that comes to my mind is of a mountain climber, determined to reach their goal, but also carrying a giant pack of heavy stones on their back, weighing them down and making every step that much harder.

For example, I see many leaders who tend to focus their energy on uncontrollable factors that they really can't do much about! These include:

- other people's behaviour
- decisions made by those in a position of authority (such as government or boards)
- big macro factors like economic, social and political events that have a knock-on effect to everything we experience.

In his classic book *The 7 Habits of Highly Effective People*, Stephen Covey talks about circles of control. His philosophy is that the most effective people do not focus their energies on the circle of 'concern' – those things that are beyond their realm of control or influence. Rather, he encourages us to focus our energy on the inner circles – on situations and events that we can either directly control or can at least influence. I've written this book with a focus on some of the most powerful things we *do* have control over; ourselves, our thought patterns and our behaviours. These are the enablers of truly effective leadership, grounded in strong self-awareness.

CASE STUDY: Sam starts to look within

When I first met Sam she struck me as someone who was deeply experienced in her field, as a well-regarded senior manager in the infrastructure industry. Not long after we met, her company went through a restructure as a result of having become acquired. As part of this process, Sam missed out on a fairly significant promotion she had presumed was coming her way. She was gutted. In our discussions, she expressed her disappointment and frustration. She was convinced the outcome was a result of gender bias and a lack of support from the executive group, including people she thought she could count on. She felt left behind and began questioning her standing in the organisation.

It took a number of weeks and several conversations to unpack how she was feeling and explore what she could do next. After a lot of reflection, Sam realised that missing out on the promotion wasn't the key issue. By focusing on factors that were outside of her control (the perceived bias and lack of support from others), she was failing to work out what would ultimately make her more satisfied with her work.

From that point, Sam started to shift her attention to what gave her the most satisfaction – leading her direct team. As she started to focus her energy in this way, she noticed the frustration and negative emotions she had been experiencing start to ease. She started to make some significant changes to how she was leading her team: addressing some of the feedback she had received in the past, slowing down and listening a lot more to what her people were saying. In the subsequent months, not only did Sam end up getting a promotion to a different role that was more suited to her, but she became far less stressed and much more satisfied in her work as a leader.

This chapter will allow you to acknowledge the real and significant external barriers you may face as a leader, while also addressing the reality of the internal barriers that may be getting in your way and causing you stress. We will also start to explore some of the most common internal barriers I've observed from working with many organisations and leaders. In doing so, I will help you to understand that these barriers are experienced by many people, that you are not alone and, most importantly, that there are practical ways to do something about them.

WHY START FROM WITHIN?

Some of the challenges you face in your work or personal life are outside of yourself – what I call external barriers. These are challenges that are getting in the way of you being able to achieve what you want, adding to your stress load, or both! They could include:

- global pandemics
- discrimination and bias
- heavy workloads
- crappy bosses
- lack of resources
- irritating or incompetent colleagues
- competing or multiple life responsibilities ... among many others!

This list of external barriers is not exhaustive nor will it apply to everyone. External factors are almost entirely out of our control and are very situational. They come and go, appear and disappear throughout our lives. Privilege (by function of socio-economics, race, gender, ability, education, geography and so on) will also mean that some people experience these barriers less than others.

These external barriers are different to the world of internal barriers – our inner world. When I say internal barriers, I don't mean mental illness or psychological or developmental disorders. I am not saying that experiencing these barriers from time to time means you are broken or that I'm diagnosing you in any way! These are common experiences, part of the human condition that affect all of us to some degree or another. It is important to start from within, because internal challenges cause you some degree of stress, and get in the way of your leadership – whether you are aware of this or not.

We need to start from within so we can be the most effective versions of ourselves as leaders, but not to the exception of agitating for change on important issues that create barriers for other people. Whatever role or background we have, the bottom line is that when we are our best and most constructive selves, we are always going to be more 'match fit' and able to tackle those persistent external barriers ourselves and others face. If we are held back by internal barriers, we cannot hope to make a difference in the world in the way that we would hope to.

There is one very important caveat I want to place here: if you are in a context that is unsafe for you, either physically or psychologically, *do not* focus within. Do not keep your energy focused on your internal barriers, when your priority should be to get yourself out of that context as soon as you are able to get help and do so. We also have to be aware of issues relating to gaslighting, where those with power and with the wrong motivations will attempt to manipulate your thoughts and cause you to feel as though the issue is with you, when it's actually being perpetrated by someone else who's out to cause you harm or elevate themselves at your expense.

My motivation with this book is to help you feel empowered and to more deeply understand yourself, not think that you are somehow faulty or 'less than'. I aim to help you identify the aspects of your thinking and behaviour that you'd like to develop over time. That point comes with an acceptance that no one has already nailed this stuff. We are all works in progress – me included! Self-awareness and continuous development are the keys to helping you achieve the leadership impact that you want to have.

Genuine self-reflection may bring you discomfort. Like many of my clients, you might find it difficult to look at yourself in the mirror honestly, especially if you are someone who works really hard at getting things 'right'. It can also be a struggle if you know what you want to change but you don't know where to start. Maybe you're worried that it's going to be too hard. That's why I've written this book – to help you learn how.

WHAT IS AN INTERNAL BARRIER?

Your internal barriers include any pervasive pattern of thought or behaviour, whether conscious or unconscious, that prevents you from achieving your leadership potential. These barriers show up regularly and tend to be patterns that are similar or consistent over time. Barriers aren't a one-time-only event where you behave in a certain way or have a particular thought and then it never happens again. The barrier may be conscious – for example, the self-talk you hear in your mind about how you are performing in a new role. Or it could be subconscious – your behaviour when you lash out at a colleague who criticised you unfairly, or unthinkingly taking on more workload than you're able to manage. You're acting without really realising what it is you are doing, or why.

Your internal barriers include any pervasive pattern of thought or behaviour, whether conscious or unconscious, that prevents you from achieving your leadership potential.

We all have these patterns as part of our wiring. Our genetic profile, personality, stage of cognitive development and life experiences shape the way we see and make sense of events. For instance, imagine giving the same feedback to two different leaders, encouraging them to contribute more creative suggestions in leadership team meetings. The differences between those two people might lead them to interpret the same feedback in completely different ways. One person might view that message as a call to action and be motivated to rise to the occasion. The other person, however, might think you don't have confidence in them, which causes them to start feeling anxious ahead of those meetings and even questioning whether they are in the right role. The key to unlocking your leadership potential is noticing and understanding any of these types of thought and behaviour patterns that are getting in the way of your potential. Once you have this awareness, the next step is to have the motivation and the tools to do something about changing those patterns ... all of which we will tackle in this book.

Leaders without self-awareness are unable to develop and grow, and ultimately are less effective because of this. Think about a leader you've worked with who has blind spots and lacks awareness of their thinking and behaviour. Maybe they assume they are strong in certain technical areas or doing really well, when in reality, they haven't earned respect from the people who work around them. If this person is never told they are missing the mark, or if they're given feedback but don't take it on board, the internal barrier will remain. They will never know that they need to take a different approach, or have the motivation to do anything differently. Development always starts with insight.

Remember my point in Chapter One, when I asked you to recall an experience of a great or terrible leader that you've worked with and what made them so. Was it all about what they knew and what they did in their job that made them great or terrible for you? Or was it about how they interacted with you and others that made the biggest difference? Ultimately, your behaviour as a leader and your interaction with others is *everything*, especially when it comes to influencing and motivating your team to do great work.

It's also helpful to remember that our behaviour is driven firstly by our thoughts, which is why it's so valuable to get a good handle on those thought patterns and understand them. Many of us have come across the iceberg model of behaviour (see the figure following). It's a psychological model for understanding the underlying causes of our behaviour in a given situation. The iceberg model reminds us that the behaviour we observe – in ourselves or others – is just the tip of the iceberg. What we don't overtly see is everything that sits below the surface: the emotional, psychological and cognitive factors that ultimately drive that behaviour we see in people. Understanding that there could be a whole raft of reasons for your peer to act like a selfish jerk, or for you to overreact to well-intended feedback, allows you to understand the source of that behaviour. To truly unlock your potential, you have to 'lift the hood' and understand the root cause of any behaviours that are getting in your way.

The iceberg model of behaviour

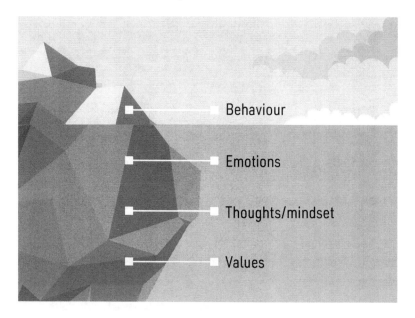

Behaviour

Emotions

Thoughts/mindset

Values

PEOPLE CAN CHANGE

My grandmother was a pretty indomitable lady who didn't mince words. She used to shake her head at people, look at me with her piercing eyes and say, 'Rearn, some people never change'. Maybe you agree with her. And to be fair, she wasn't wrong! But just because *some* people never change, isn't to say that people *can't* change. People can become self-aware through regular reflection and with the help of others – whether that's a coach, a great boss or a trusted (and honest) friend.

Everything we have learned about neuroplasticity and the ability for the brain to develop tells us that we can and do evolve our thought patterns and behaviours. In his groundbreaking book

The Brain That Changes Itself, psychiatrist Norman Doidge tells the story of a woman who became blind and subsequently developed the ability to speed 'read' audio books at an astounding rate. He theorised this was a result of her brain's auditory processing taking over what was previously her visual processing function. The ability for our brains to evolve – through either conscious effort or 'rewiring', as we will explore later, or through unconscious adaptive mechanisms – is a shining source of optimism when it comes to thinking about our potential growth as humans.

Obviously, not all thought and behaviour patterns will get in your way. Lots of them are constructive, and will actually enable your success as a leader. A good example is having a growth mindset, the pattern of thinking defined by American psychologist and author Carol Dweck as believing 'that our most basic abilities can be developed through dedication and hard work. This view creates a love of learning and a resilience that is essential for great accomplishment'. Obviously this is a thought pattern that will help to set you up for success.

So, how can you work out which internal barriers *aren't* helping you succeed? Start becoming aware of which thoughts and behaviour patterns are preventing you from achieving your leadership potential *or* affecting your wellbeing. This starts with tuning in to your self-talk – the patterns of thoughts that are going through your mind. Learn to listen to what you are saying to yourself. Is that talk positive, negative, distracting, depleting or lifting you up? As you prepare for that big meeting that's coming up, as you take on a new task you've never done before, as you respond to a frustrated stakeholder: learn to tune in to what you are saying to yourself at that moment. Listen to your self-talk like a radio station or a podcast, without necessarily judging it at this point or trying to change anything.

A great way to access your thinking is to write your thoughts down using a journal, or even use a recorder tool like Rev to articulate your self-talk out loud and listen back to it. It might be confronting at first, but becoming aware of your self-talk helps you notice where you are focusing most of your mental energy and the impact that has on your emotions and behaviour.

REFLECT AFTER THE FACT

If I had to identify a single factor that most helps leaders to unlock their potential, my vote would be the skill and habit of reflection. As American psychologist and educational reformer John Dewey said, 'We do not learn from experience. We learn from reflecting on experience.' I encourage you to build self-awareness by practising reflection, *after the fact*.

'We do not learn from experience. We learn from reflecting on experience.' – John Dewey

Let's say you just had an interaction at work and you noticed something particular about your behaviour. Perhaps it was the way that you communicated or how you responded. Perhaps it felt a bit off, or your words didn't quite land the way you wanted. Reflecting after the fact means to pause and think about your response in that situation, as well as the outcome that followed that response. To help you think about these steps more clearly, the diagram below shows a four-step cycle of reflection that I've adapted from the educationalist David Kolb's model of experiential learning.

Four-step cycle of reflection

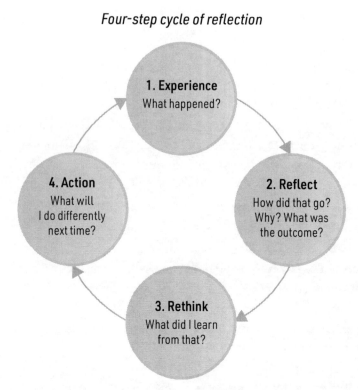

Over time, with a regular practice of reflection, you should start to notice patterns, triggers or events that prompt you to behave in a certain way. Another way to become aware of your behaviour patterns is by seeking out and listening to feedback from others. We'll explore that later in the book.

Through reflection and with the help of good-quality feedback, ask yourself: is this behavioural pattern something that you are proud of, that makes you feel good and that is achieving good outcomes? Or does the behavioural pattern feel a bit 'off', going against the grain of who you really are or want to be, or not achieving the outcomes you are seeking?

At this point, maybe you're not quite sure yet what your patterns look like, or perhaps you know immediately what they are but you're not sure you can change them. That's entirely okay. This book will help you pinpoint what those patterns are for you, and show you practical ways to shift them over time.

THE COSTS THAT COME

When you are held back by your internal barriers, it costs you: either in terms of your physical and mental wellbeing – such as stress, worry or ill health – or in your ability to achieve positive outcomes in your work. It can also cost you in terms of the unintended impact you have on those around you when you're not at your best as a leader. Being aware of these costs can help you become motivated to do something about it.

These costs may be immediate and obvious – for example, feeling sick and anxious after someone's critique of you. The costs may be relatively minor – for example, needing to put in longer hours for a few weeks because you unconsciously took on more work than you really should have. Or the costs could be very significant – you could develop a physiological issue or chronic stress, or you may have to step back from leadership altogether as a result of burnout. Burnout levels are higher than ever before, particularly for female leaders since the beginning of the COVID-19 pandemic. According to McKinsey's 'Women in the Workplace 2021' report, female leaders report higher levels of chronic stress, exhaustion and burnout than men. These levels increase as the women become more senior, with over 40 per cent of senior leaders surveyed reporting burnout and exhaustion.

These barriers don't feel good but, more importantly, they also impair your productivity and get in the way of your optimal functioning. Your mental and physical health should always take priority. It's like putting the oxygen mask on yourself first as a leader. And it's not just you who can be affected. It's also your work outcomes, the impact you have on others and, potentially, your career that can be negatively impacted.

Learning the hard way

Eight years ago I was working in the financial services sector. I had just returned from my first period of parental leave to take on a more senior role in my function. That would have been a stretch in itself, but I was also experiencing all of the common challenges of returning to work as a first-time parent. I was feeling upset about leaving my son in childcare especially as he was experiencing separation anxiety. I was missing him and feeling like I wasn't doing a good job either at being a parent or in my new role. I was also experiencing a number of external barriers – including a pretty tough workplace culture. The thought patterns I was experiencing at that time were telling me that I didn't have what it took to be a working parent, that I didn't know how to do this new job, that I wasn't doing well enough in my work and that I was letting everyone down.

I didn't express any of those internal thoughts to anyone except my husband for many months. While I kept going to work and doing my job, the effect of months of that internal noise was that I started to become sick. I was experiencing headaches. My immune system suffered. I started to lose energy and have disrupted sleep patterns. I became teary and emotional in the workplace, which was very unlike me. After several months, it reached a point where I fully bottomed out. I had lost all sense of confidence in my abilities.

By the time I finally shared some of the thoughts I'd been having with my manager, they were so shocked to discover this was how I was feeling. I had done such a good job of continuing to show up without giving any glimpse into what I was experiencing internally. As hard as they then tried to help me undo some of that thinking and convince me to stay, the damage was done and I made the choice to leave. I learned a valuable lesson – the internal barriers can be insidious and can do us a great deal of damage, even when we are aware of them.

 UNLOCKED TIPS

Even if you aren't yet feeling the cost of these barriers at this point in time, I encourage you to have practices in place to help you self-monitor. Specifically, I encourage you to monitor for when your wellbeing is affected or when you start to feel like work is taking its toll. The COVID-19 pandemic taught us all a lot about self-care. If this is something you occasionally struggle with, you can monitor your wellbeing by keeping an eye on all the signs that show up for you when you are feeling pressure or strain. For many people, the initial signs are often physical. They can include affected sleep patterns; heavier reliance on substances like coffee, sugar or alcohol; a lack of motivation to do the things that you would normally enjoy or that you know are good for you; headaches; colds or other sicknesses; and affected appetite. I always get a sore throat first – it's a sure-fire sign that I'm not in a good space and need to slow down.

What if the costs you are monitoring relate more to your career? Notice any signs that could signal that something's getting in the way of your leadership effectiveness. You may not get the performance evaluation that you hoped for, or maybe you were passed over for a new role or an opportunity that you felt confident about securing. Maybe some of your work relationships aren't as strong as they were or could be. These all indicate potential blind spots in how others perceive your leadership at this point in time, and it's critical that you bring them into your awareness. The key to overcoming these blind spots is asking for feedback, which we'll explore later in the book.

When it comes to your wellbeing, you won't always get the balance right. We all experience periods of our lives when we find ourselves in a 'good patch', when we feel confident and seem to be going along well on all fronts. Then we might hit a rough period – we're faced with enormous demands, our health starts to slip, we start questioning ourselves, or we're achieving so much that we actually start overdoing it. There will be cycles of high times and low times, and sometimes the gap between those cycles can last a long time or they can switch up really quickly! The key is to be aware and look for the warning signs that you might be hitting that rough patch, so you can start to do something about it.

YOU ARE NOT ALONE

Your experience may feel lonely if it seems that you are the only one facing these internal barriers. Yet they exist similarly for leaders from all walks of life, across industries, levels of experience and backgrounds. A big part of the challenge is that we don't talk much about our difficulties, so you might wrongly assume that others aren't experiencing the same things that you are. There's also cognitive bias in action – the assumption that you're the only one like this and that others are different to you. Knowing that you're not the only one who experiences these challenges helps to normalise them. It can also empower you, because if you know that others can overcome these challenges, perhaps you can too (spoiler alert: you can!).

Through the many conversations I've had with leaders over 20 years, I've seen consistent patterns that have finally led me to write this book. I've facilitated hundreds of sessions with groups of leaders and asked them to share what they find difficult, only to consistently see their surprise and often relief when they learn that others around them are experiencing similar things.

As you explore the patterns I describe in this book, you might feel like your challenges or internal barriers are a bit different to what I describe. I completely accept that you may have specific patterns that don't quite fit with some of the stories and examples I share in this book. If this is the case, I encourage you to use the golden principles that I'm describing, that can apply to everyone:

1. Be clear on the leadership impact you want to have.

2. Become aware of any recurring thought and behaviour patterns.

3. Reflect. Consider how these patterns are impacting you or others. Are they getting in the way? How?

4. Seek support or learning to help you adjust these patterns over time, using the principles of staying unlocked that we will cover in Chapter Eight.

IT STARTS – AND ENDS – WITH YOU

Knowing you are not alone means you are not broken or 'less than', and that all of your day-to-day experiences of internal barriers are totally, utterly normal. It makes you human! At the same time, if you truly want to find your best leadership, you must work out if these patterns are getting in your way, and then have the motivation to do something about it. The rest of this book is dedicated to helping you rewire these patterns effectively.

Before you dive into learning about the barriers and what you can do differently, it's important to remember that you're a continuous work in progress – as is everyone else. This work of developing as a leader is never really finished, never perfected, never mastered – much like our work as parents, friends and human beings. You will go through cycles of feeling like you are nailing this leadership stuff and overcoming those old barriers, quickly followed by moments when you doubt your growth and feel like the old patterns are rearing their heads again.

Bottom line: when it comes to your own leadership growth, own it. Truly know that this journey starts and ends (but doesn't really end!) with you. Only you can be held accountable for taking action on what are ultimately your thoughts and behaviours. No one else can do this work for you. But you and everyone around you will benefit when you do.

FROM STARTING WITHIN, TO UNDERSTANDING

Despite the many external challenges you face as a leader, by starting within you can bring deeper awareness to the patterns that are working for you, and those that are getting in your way.

Understand you are not alone in experiencing them, and that you can overcome them by using the tools I share in this book.

What I most want for you is to start identifying which patterns are getting in the way of you unlocking your potential as a leader.

Now that you know you must start within, let's look at how these internal barriers work, so that you can start to do something about them.

CHAPTER THREE

Moving to Awareness

By becoming aware of the specific barriers that are getting in your way, you can create new patterns of thinking and behaviour that will best serve you and others. Understanding how you think helps you to operate more effectively as a leader. Knowing why you behave the way you do helps you become the leader you really want to be. Making the connection between your thoughts and behaviours and the resulting outcomes allows you to identify the changes you want to make to achieve different outcomes in the future.

With a deep awareness of the type of leader you really want to be and the impact you want to have in the world, you can align your thinking and behaviours to achieve those outcomes. Specifically, this means consciously articulating your goals, not just in practical terms but in terms of the impact you want to have on the people around you. This is what I mean by becoming the leader you are meant to be – not someone else's idea of who they think you should be, which is always biased. It's becoming the leader that you *want* to be and believe deep down that you *can* be.

Understanding the connection between how you think, feel and behave is the only way to see your actions clearly and understand their source. Without this insight you won't understand where to start with your development – you'll be shooting in the dark. And you won't grow or unlock your potential as a leader.

Understanding the connection between how you think, feel and behave is the only way to see your actions clearly.

CASE STUDY: Ahmed makes some realisations

I met Ahmed several years ago as part of a senior leadership team session I was running. He was an experienced leader who had been in the business for a number of years, and considered to be an expert in his field of operations.

As I worked with the team to help them achieve their goal of becoming a more cohesive and high-performing group, each member was tasked with thinking about their behaviour as part of the team and the impact this had on the team dynamic.

When I met with each of the leaders one-on-one, most demonstrated an understanding of their strengths and gaps, reflecting on some of their behaviours that might have contributed to tension in the group. Ahmed was the only one who couldn't make this connection. He was a passionate person who cared a lot about his work. He described his love for his family and that he wanted to make them proud by achieving success in his career. He had aspirations of becoming his boss's successor. He had good intentions, a smart mind and loads of experience.

However, Ahmed was so busy keeping up with the demands of his workload that he was not taking the time to consider the impact of his behaviour on the rest of the team. The 360-degree feedback he received from his boss (the CEO) and his peers said he was talented, but that he could also be brash and domineering and usually assumed he had the right answer.

The impact of this behaviour was that team meetings often resulted in conflict, with others not having as much opportunity to contribute. As a result, he was losing credibility and his peers' trust. Unfortunately, he didn't know this was how he was seen. From his own perspective, all he was trying to do was get a good outcome for the business. Through our ongoing conversations, he realised that, deep down, he wanted his boss to know that he had good ideas and was capable of taking on the CEO role in the future.

Through the feedback process and coaching conversations, Ahmed started to make the connection between his thinking (wanting to demonstrate his value) and his behaviour (pushing others aside and dominating the team). But more than this: he also started to see a disconnect between what he wanted to achieve (the CEO role) and the actual impact he was having (eroding his credibility and the trust others had in him). That recognition was the turning point for him. He started to become conscious of when and how he contributed to team discussions. He started listening more and asking more questions, instead of rushing in to provide his opinions before others had a chance. As a result, his behaviour became more aligned with the outcomes he wanted to see happen. He started earning back the respect of his boss and peers. He created more space for others on the team to contribute. He also realised he didn't have to be the one with all the answers.

This chapter will help you discover whether you're having the impact you *really* want to have as a leader; to understand if you are operating in 'auto mode'; and to work out how others see your leadership right now.

WHEN THERE IS TOO MUCH GOING ON

When you are living at pace, managing the full demands of work and your personal life coupled with the rapidly changing world, it can be difficult to think objectively and act with awareness from moment to moment. I do not know a single person who isn't struggling at times to keep up with their life and workload. You will know firsthand the pressures that come from living and working within the hectic pace of the world around you.

Living this way makes it hard for leaders to think clearly and to ensure that they're working towards the right things. It is all of these external demands, combined with the internal barriers that I describe in this book, that pull you into a state where it can be difficult to think objectively and with self-awareness. This creates two problems. Firstly, you aren't always able to step back and think clearly about what you're trying to achieve. Secondly, you tend not to notice whether you're on track towards achieving those important outcomes.

Whatever your individual circumstances – you could be an executive with pressure from the board and constantly booked with meetings, a working parent with multiple demands on your time and energy, or an aspiring leader with loads to offer who is trying to keep up with others' expectations and learn as you go – you'll face a similar challenge of having so much to do every day. Learning how to extract yourself from that busyness is critical for your ability to think clearly.

As with our case study, Ahmed, you are undoubtedly working hard and doing your best in your role. Consider, though, whether the hard work, long hours and effort is working towards the outcomes you want to achieve. Unfortunately, your efforts may not always result in the impact you intend – though not through lack of trying! In the sections that follow, I will invite you to think about the impact you want to have as a leader. I'll prompt you to think not only about what is important to you, but also what those around you expect and need from your leadership. Being clear on your intentions is like setting up goalposts – it gives you something clear to aim for, and then evaluate your efforts against.

WHAT ARE YOUR INTENTIONS?

There may be times when you get lucky. Your leadership efforts may happily align with what others need and the impact you have is exactly what you intend. I call that unconscious alignment. But when the context we are in changes so rapidly, the ability to stop, reflect and reset so that your impact is still aligned with your intention is a key skill. It's what will make the difference between being lucky and being a great leader.

A big part of this is to define the impact that you want to have in two ways:

1. *Tangible outcomes.* What are the outcomes or the achievements that you want to realise? They could include financial targets, delivery of projects, developing a product, building a team or other tangible deliverables.

2. *Felt impact.* What is the felt impact of your leadership that you want to create? How do you want people around you to think, feel or behave as a result of your interactions with them? A consideration here might be the values that you want to operate by and be known for.

At this point, I really want you to pause and take some time to think about these questions. In my experience, this is the first part of the puzzle that most leaders don't spend enough time getting right. Take the time now to think about your answers to these two questions. Jot down some notes. Read them again. They should *really* inspire and motivate you. If they don't, try again. You want to be super clear about what matters most to you and others, before you head off down that track.

EVALUATION IS ESSENTIAL

At the end of a work day, take a quiet 15 minutes to look back at these notes you made about your leadership intentions and evaluate as honestly as possible using the following questions:

- How much time did you spend working towards the tangible achievements that you want to achieve?
- How much alignment was there between your actual behaviour and the felt impact you want to have on those around you?

On average, aim for at least 50 per cent alignment between your time spent, actual behaviour and those intentions. If it's less, that's not a fail mark. You'll always have days, weeks or perhaps even months where you find yourself off track with how you want to be leading. There are lots of reasons for that. It may be fatigue. There may be challenges in your personal life. You might be in learning mode or out of your comfort zone in a new role or situation that you're dealing with. It's always good to notice that lack of alignment, though. You can spend some time thinking about what led you off track, then quickly course-correct and reset those intentions as you push on ahead.

You might not yet be in the habit of reflecting on these things because it requires you to look hard at yourself, and question whether the effort you are putting in is truly paying off. When you're working so hard, that's a difficult question to honestly ask yourself. But it's absolutely worth it if you want to lead with intention.

AUTO MODE DOESN'T WORK

Reacting in auto mode, especially in a threat state, pretty much guarantees you will face problems in your work and with the people around you. You probably have a good understanding of what happens to the brain when you're in a situation that you perceive to be a threat. The human brain is brilliant at lots of things but it isn't great at distinguishing between physical threats (like a predatory animal approaching) and social threats (like when your peers criticise your work in front of others).

The iceberg model explains the connection between your thoughts, how those thoughts make you feel and how you subsequently behave. When you react automatically to a situation you deem to be a threat, you're shifted from thoughts straight into behaviour. That can take the form of what is known as flight or fight mode.

When we're in flight mode, we model behaviours like running away or avoiding difficult people or situations that make us uncomfortable. Behaviourally, it can include staying quiet or holding back in a meeting. In contrast, when we see fight mode in action that can involve things like slamming doors, shooting off colourful emails in the heat of the moment, lashing out or criticising the other person.

Both of these modes can create problems such as damage to your brand as a leader, strain on the relationships with people around you or derailing the outcomes you're trying to achieve. If you pause to become aware of your emotional state, you can then choose a more constructive response that will lead to a better outcome.

Many of us have worked for (suffered!) a boss who was totally unpredictable with a tendency to fly off the handle, avoid all the tough stuff and make life generally awful for everyone around them. People want leaders who are able to choose a measured response that is going to create better outcomes for the organisation, for the team and for themselves. By doing this, you'll be a leader who is more consistent, more reliable and able to get the best out of the people you work with.

CASE STUDY: Selena is in flight mode

Selena was a bright and highly driven corporate counsel with a not-for-profit organisation. She was also the only female on the executive team, having recently been promoted to her first senior leadership role.

A few months into her new role, I asked her how she was experiencing the transition into the team. Despite her excitement at the opportunity, Selena openly shared that she was in a constant state of stress whenever she was in meetings with her peers. Interestingly, this was not the case when she was with her own team of direct reports.

As I probed further to understand what was happening, she described how, in executive team meetings, she didn't contribute on any issues that sat outside her area of expertise. When we explored this, Selena realised that her reluctance to contribute was due to her concern that her peers would criticise her for not being 'commercial' enough, or that she might say something that would make her look silly or inexperienced. She only saw threat in those situations, and her behaviour reflected a flight-mode reaction, which caused her to stay quiet.

It took a number of follow up conversations with her managing director before Selena began to understand the importance of her role as an equal, contributing member of the executive leadership team. By identifying her fears and pushing herself to speak up more on broader organisational issues, Selena gradually proved to herself that her value extended beyond her specific field of technical expertise.

Fight mode is in all of us

You will have seen many examples of high-profile leaders in fight mode. Perhaps you can recall your own moments operating in this mode, too. One recent example that comes to my mind is an Australian Football League (AFL) head coach who was challenged by a media journalist about his team's rostering in a particular round and a suspected leak from within the club regarding this issue. It's fair to say the journalist went outside the typical playbook in the way that he was asking the questions, but it was technically in alignment with what he was there to do.

The behaviour shown by the head coach in response was striking. His face coloured red; his eyes grew wide. He started gesturing angrily to the journalist to get up and leave. He challenged him on his professional integrity. He called him names. Eventually, seeing that no other option was seemingly left available to him, the coach stormed out. As a result, he immediately faced backlash in the media for what was seen as an unprofessional overreaction. The next day he subsequently issued an apology and the club gave a $20,000 donation to a charity as a gesture of goodwill.

I share this as an example rather than a criticism, as I don't know the exact circumstances or what the coach was thinking and feeling at that moment. However, I can make some connections and suggest that he perhaps viewed the journalist's questions as being out of line with his own sense of fairness; as a challenge to his own effectiveness as a coach; and/or as exposing a potential weakness of his organisation. In fight mode, that coach lost his composure and missed an opportunity to respond with measured comments that would have made his point without the resulting damage.

You might think that sometimes you just need people to see and hear how you *really* feel. I'm all for being authentic, but there is a big difference between thoughtfully communicating how you feel versus firing off a response. In the former, you are pausing to consider what message you want to give the person, why that message is important to you and what you want to see happen next. This is the difference between being constructive, as compared to not being at your best.

🔓 UNLOCKED TIPS

Whenever you feel emotion taking over your judgement, pause. Take a deep breath. That simple act will re-engage your prefrontal cortex, which is associated with logic and holds your executive decision-making functions. This will make it easier for you to maintain your composure.

Then consider what next act is most aligned with the leader you want to be in this moment. Ask yourself:

- What is upsetting me about this situation?
- What am I really worried about?
- Am I concerned or fearful of anything here?
- If I want this moment to reflect who I am, what should my next action be?

Then, when you feel ready to respond, there are some phrases that might help you to stay in the constructive zone:

- 'Can you tell me a bit more about that?' or 'Can you help me understand this more?' (This buys you time before you respond, and might give you more information to work with.)
- 'I hear that you are concerned about ...' (This allows you to acknowledge the other person and show that you are actively listening.)
- 'At this point, my view is ...' (This provides the equivalent of a 'Yes, and ...' It allows you to build on the conversation constructively without escalating the tension. It also signals that your point of view may potentially change on the basis of further information, which demonstrates your flexibility.)

- 'What if we were to …' (This brings you and the other person into the same realm to consider a different, future-focused possibility that could achieve mutual benefit. It invites them to be part of a solution with you.)

There may also be an option of temporarily pausing the interaction until you are in a better state to address and resolve the issue. Some phrases to use here could include:

- 'I understand this is an important issue to resolve.'
- 'There's a lot here for me to consider.'
- 'At this moment, I don't think that we are in the best state to resolve this.'
- 'I'm going to take some time to think, and then let's continue this discussion at …' (It's important to be specific and not allow too much time to pass – ideally follow it up within the next 24 hours, if you can.)

With this approach, it's important to note two things. Firstly, you will not always have the option of walking away from an interaction. But if the situation is becoming wildly unconstructive with signs of disrespect or even aggression, that's a good signal that the conversation should be halted until you and the other person have regained composure.

Secondly, it's important to not feel like you have to apologise for calling 'time out'. This is not a failure; it's a conscious choice to pause the conversation until you're able to continue constructively. You are not running away from it as long as you follow through on your commitment to continue that conversation as you've indicated.

It's not easy

There are several factors that can make it difficult to halt our auto-mode reactions, one of which is fatigue. Running at pace, dealing with a crazy workload, endless meetings, resource constraints … no wonder we get tired. There are no short answers or quick fixes to combat fatigue, but we do know what can help – practising self-care, engaging in conscious rest and taking micro breaks throughout the day. A micro break is a one-minute pause between meetings, conversations, phone calls or emails, where you focus on your breathing and clear your mind. It allows your brain to reset. I find micro breaks to be achievable and helpful for leaders who are scheduled back-to-back with barely any time to breathe in their days. While they might not completely re-energise you, micro breaks are a good hack to help bring back some of the energy into your prefrontal cortex so you can better self-regulate.

Another common cause for an auto-mode reaction is when our personal values are being compromised by someone else's behaviour – especially if it's someone who holds very different values to our own. I'm not suggesting that you should change your values to avoid being triggered. On the contrary, you should embrace those values and at the same time be aware of their influence on your behaviour. If you're not sure what your values are and would like to become a bit more familiar with them, try using an online tool such as the Personal Values Assessment (PVA).

To help you understand what usually triggers your values and prompts a reaction (read: what makes you upset!), answer this question: 'One thing that people do that always upsets me is …'. For me, it's when people are intentionally unkind to others. Knowing what yours is helps you to be on the lookout. When you see that behaviour in others, you will know it can be a trigger for you and will possibly send you into auto mode. You'll already be on alert (in a good way), so you can be ready to pause and regulate your response in a constructive manner.

HOW DO PEOPLE REALLY SEE YOU?

Edward de Bono, the renowned psychologist, expert thinking teacher and author of *Six Thinking Hats,* was quoted as saying, 'Perception is real, even when it is not reality.' You shouldn't assume that just because you *intend* to lead in a certain way, and are trying really hard to lead in that way, that others will *perceive* you in that same way. If you want to ensure you are having the impact that you intend, you have to seek confirmation – ask and find out the perception others have of your leadership. If they're not seeing the behaviours or actions you're trying hard to show, you aren't having the actual impact that you're seeking to have. Your impact is ultimately about how other people experience you.

> **'Perception is real, even when it is not reality.'**
> – Edward de Bono

The feedback you need versus the feedback you receive

In my experience, not many leaders have an accurate, detailed and current understanding of how they are seen by the people around them. When I conduct feedback conversations with leaders, there is usually at least some degree of surprise when they hear the full story of how others really see them. The reasons for this may include:

- they are too busy to invest time in seeking or acting on feedback

- they avoid seeking feedback as it can be confronting to ask for and receive
- they assume they already know how people see them
- they don't care
- they have asked, but have only been given part of the story!

Despite your efforts to ask for feedback, the people around you may decide it is not in their best interests to provide you with honest feedback, yet you may be operating on the assumption that they have. This creates blind spots. You may be carrying on in your current mode, thinking you're all on track, but in reality you may be losing the ability to influence or motivate those around you – or, worse, doing real damage to your relationships and your brand as a leader.

If you don't have a current, honest view of how your leadership is perceived, you could be missing opportunities to know what you're doing well (so you know what to keep doing!), as well as what you're not doing so well. Receiving honest feedback doesn't mean you have to be what people want all the time, but at least you will understand what their view is, so you can make an informed decision about what you do next.

We've all seen many examples of leaders operating with blind spots. One of the classic causes of this is when leaders consciously surround themselves with 'yes' people. Think of the various world leaders over the course of history who consciously chose to gather people around them who would provide lip service and tell them only what they wanted to hear! Even if you don't go out of your way to create a bubble around you, it can still happen unintentionally – and it means you miss out on the whole story.

CASE STUDY: Loretta finds her blind spots

Loretta was a committed, passionate and (by her own admission!) slightly perfectionistic leader in the education system who had recently stepped into her first senior school leadership role. Several months into her tenure, Loretta came under significant pressure from the school board. They had concerns that her leadership team were not fully engaged, which in their mind presented retention and reputation risks.

When the board raised their concerns, Loretta felt totally confused – and a just a bit defensive. She prided herself on her commitment to her team and felt that she was consistently supportive of them. In all of her recent one-on-one conversations her team members expressed satisfaction and told her to 'just keep doing what she was doing'. As it turned out, in reality, half of her team members were not giving her their honest perspective – they felt she was playing favourites and showed bias towards the peers who held longer tenure at the school.

Eventually, the deputy principal in her team chose to step in as a circuit-breaker because of all the disgruntled noise he was hearing from his peers. He told Loretta directly what she hadn't seen until now: that half of her team did not feel comfortable or motivated to give her the whole story. As confronting as it was for her to hear this, and even though it was never her intention to create this issue, finally seeing the whole story gave Loretta a valuable opportunity to shift her behaviour and create the team environment she needed.

I often hear from people who despairingly say to me, 'But I *do* ask for feedback! I can't force people to tell me what they don't want to. At least I'm asking.' While asking for feedback is an important and great first step, it won't guarantee you get the whole story of how people see you. Let's look at the ways you can do this.

TAKE YOUR MEDICINE

I remember being given cod liver oil off a spoon as a child by my well-meaning grandparents, who were convinced it would keep me healthy and aid my recovery from colds. Who knows, it probably did. But it was terrible. I used to dread it. My stomach would squirm in anticipation, and I would grimace and root my feet to the floor to avoid the temptation to flee (I was a pretty dutiful kid, otherwise I probably would have!). And yet I logically understood that this short experience – however unpleasant – was going to be helpful to me.

I think of feedback in the same way.

You may have had negative experiences with feedback in the past. Perhaps you've received feedback that was difficult to hear, unexpected or terribly delivered – and now you've (understandably) got a bit of an aversion. If this is the case, remember that the only way to avoid this same outcome in the future is to do something differently. Nothing ventured, nothing gained.

You may be fearful of what you will be told when you ask. This is a totally normal flight mode reaction. It's also the equivalent of sticking your head in the sand. It is always better to know the truth and be in a position to do something about it than to avoid reality and end up further away from the leader you want to be. And showing people that you are committed to becoming a better leader and that you value their point of view only helps to build trust between you.

You might simply feel you are too busy, or worry that you'll seem self-doubting by asking for feedback. But remember the value that comes from operating with awareness. Your success as a leader depends on it. It's a good investment of your time, made even more worthwhile when you know *how* to ask for feedback.

 UNLOCKED TIPS

Here are my top tips for asking for feedback; they'll give you the best chance of receiving an honest and constructive response:

1. *Ask for feedback on your leadership regularly.* It can't be a once-a-year event. Situations around us are changing quickly, and there will likely be new people coming in and out of your stakeholder groups. It's not about seeking validation on a constant basis! But I would recommend an informal check-in fairly regularly (ideally every couple of months), especially those with whom you work closely.

2. *Seek feedback from diverse perspectives.* Consider the 360-degree view – your direct reports, manager/s, team members, cross-functional peers and clients. Avoid the trap that many fall into (and I've been guilty of myself!) which is to only ask for feedback from the same one person with whom you are comfortable. Our subconscious is sneaky and wants to protect our ego, hence we tend to ask people with whom we have a good relationship. Adam Grant, psychologist and author of

the book *Think Again,* says we should use a 'challenger network' by deliberately reaching out to people we know will challenge our thinking, including how we think about our own leadership.

3. *Tell others which leadership areas you are working on.* For instance, share with your manager or team that you are committed to improving your delegating skills, or becoming more inclusive. Not only will this enable the other person to give you relevant feedback on this area, but it might also spur them to mention any *other* areas they feel you could develop that you may not have considered.

4. *Be specific with your feedback-seeking.* This will likely encourage people to be more honest with you (and maybe inspire them to seek feedback of their own). Ask open questions that are future-focused. For example, 'At the moment I'm trying to focus on ... What feedback could you give me about how I'm going with this? What could I do differently to get better?' If you want feedback from your direct reports, you could say: 'In what way can I better support your growth/performance? What can I do more or less of? What am I not doing currently that would really help you?'

5. *Thank them and take action.* It's important to thank people for their feedback (or at least acknowledge you have heard them), let them know that you will give it real consideration and then (ideally!) take the relevant action to show you are committed to your ongoing development.

COURSE-CORRECTING AS YOU GO

Being clear on your intended impact, pausing to respond rather than react and seeking out regular honest feedback means that you will be empowered to continuously develop. You'll know how others truly perceive you and whether the impact you are having is aligned with how you intend to lead. This allows you to make more regular, minor 'course corrections' in your behaviours and leadership style, rather than waiting until there are much larger and more serious gaps between what you intend, what others need and the reality of how you are currently leading. None of us want to be there.

By course-correcting, you can be more aligned with who you want to be as a leader, create a more positive impact on others and set a constructive example to those around you. You can potentially avoid those horrible, distressing moments in your career where you're blindsided by feedback you did not see coming.

You've probably had moments in your career where you've had an unexpected wake-up call or a moment of realisation. Think about a time when you were given surprising feedback – perhaps good, or perhaps not so great – and realised you weren't perceived the way that you thought you were. Maybe you had food stuck in your teeth in a meeting and no one told you. Or maybe it was something more significant – for instance, you thought you were making it safe for everyone in your team to contribute their ideas, until someone finally pointed out that you never took the time to ask them. The point is that these moments of realisation happen to all of us, and they are super valuable. As a leader you should go after them like a heat-seeking missile!

Who is holding the compass?

I've had conversations with leaders who reach a point of thinking, 'Wouldn't it be best if I just focused on what I'm trying to achieve, rather than being worried about what others think of me all the time?' But leadership doesn't exist in isolation of others. As a leader you have to consider both what you want to achieve, and what others see as success in your role as leader. It's a 'both-and' situation.

Of course, there will be times when you need to be more self-determined and single-minded in regard to your leadership, when others' views will bear less significance and importance. A powerful example is if you choose to go against social expectations or take a stand on a particular issue you care about, for a specific and intentional reason. Think of the inspirational Grace Tame. In 2021, at the conclusion of her term as Australian of the Year, Tame was invited to meet with former prime minister Scott Morrison. In a very public and high-profile moment that was built up by the media, Tame was photographed as she awkwardly shook hands, unsmiling, with Morrison in what some considered to be against the typical etiquette or social norms involved in meeting someone who holds a significant position of power.

That behaviour was clearly intentional. Tame later stated that she did not feel compelled to act in a certain way for a person she did not respect, and who did nothing to earn her respect. She faced significant public support but also fallout from some in the public sphere because her behaviour was not aligned with societal expectations.

Without question, this was a leadership moment. It is defined as such by the fact that this was someone who set a clear intention and acted in alignment with that intention. Tame consciously chose that action based on personal values and beliefs that she was not prepared to compromise, and I'm betting she did so while hoping her behaviour would lead to positive change.

For those of us mere mortals doing our day jobs, we can be inspired by this example but should also be aware that choosing to move against the grain usually comes at some degree of cost to our status in the eyes of people who won't like our stance. That may be something that you are comfortable to accept as a trade-off for upholding your values or bringing about the positive change you are seeking to achieve. If so, go for it.

Am I on track?

I reacquainted myself with running during COVID-19. It was my strategy for dealing with a crappy situation and a way to practise self-care. I ran with an awesome friend who was a lot fitter and more experienced than I was. We would set off faithfully every Sunday. There was always a moment at the beginning of the run when we had to decide on our destination for the day. Was it going to be a leisurely 5 kilometres along the flat riverside track? Or were we going to push ourselves and go for 14 kilometres up and down hills?

At various points on the run, we would check in with each other. How are you finding it? Is this too fast? Do you want to pick up the pace? Do you want to change routes and take the uphill track? Am I talking too much and do you want me to be quiet? Checking in with each other in this way would mean that sometimes we ended up at a different destination from the one we'd originally decided on. But by setting our intention first and then checking in as we went along, it was always a much more mutually satisfying outcome than if one person had set the destination and forced the other to follow (limping and gasping) along.

 UNLOCKED TIPS

In your leadership role, consider what you're aiming for right now. Review the notes you made earlier about your intentions: statements about what you want to achieve, the impact you want to have on others and what it will look like when this happens. Keep these intention statements somewhere close and review them – at first weekly, then monthly – as part of your commitment to regularly course-correct. Have a hard think about whether your intentions are serving you and others.

Ask for feedback along the way and get that valuable input from others – both on what you are trying to achieve and whether or not the journey to get there is working for those around you. Do you need to slow down or go faster or take a different route? Continuing to get that information will allow you to make minor course corrections before you end up wildly off track.

As you're taking this approach with your team, let them know what you are doing. Be explicit about it. You could say things like, 'I'm charting the course here, but I want your input to confirm where our destination is, what route we should take, and how fast or slow we should go. And I'm going to keep getting your data along the way.' That sends an important signal to them that, while you are the leader, their input and feedback is crucial and valued.

STAYING ON TRACK

The most effective leaders regularly consider the impact they want to have and respond consciously and with awareness in a range of situations. They seek out and use feedback to know how they are *(really)* being perceived. They also make conscious choices about what to do differently next time, so they can regularly course-correct and stay on track towards their goals.

We've now explored this type of intentional leadership and how some of the internal barriers work. In the next chapter, I'm going to introduce the three most common leadership patterns I've observed. Each of these patterns affects leaders in different but equally significant ways. Throughout the rest of this book, I will help you understand how these patterns develop, what they look like in action, how to identify them in yourself (and others!) and – most importantly – what to do about them.

CHAPTER FOUR

Going Fast, Holding Back, Overdoing

It goes without question: we're individuals, each with our own unique blueprint of genetic influences, experiences, values and outlooks on life. That uniqueness is valuable and something to be thoughtfully woven into how you lead, every day. For that reason, I'll never suggest that we should pigeonhole anyone into a narrow box, nor give them a prescriptive set of rules to follow to successfully lead. The task of leadership is way too complex, as are we as humans.

With this acknowledged, over many years and countless interactions with leaders I've observed a consistent set of overarching patterns. These patterns include:

- how leaders *think* (how they see situations and what goes through their minds – their interpretations, beliefs, self-talk and assumptions)

- how leaders *behave* (what they do, how they interact with others, the decisions they make, how they communicate).

These patterns are clearly observable to others as a result of their behaviour, but they become especially clear when the person steps back to reflect on their thoughts and behaviours, and shares those reflections with others. These patterns are also reflected in data from millions of psychometric and leadership assessments completed globally every year, which identify and describe leaders' thoughts and behaviours in the workplace.

Throughout this chapter (and with further detail in Chapters Five to Seven), I will share with you the three different patterns I have observed. I'll bring them to life with examples and descriptions of how these thoughts and behaviours show up in the workplace, and the associated impact of these patterns on others.

I define the patterns as:

- Going Fast
- Holding Back
- Overdoing.

I know from firsthand experience and my understanding of psychology that it can be difficult to see your own thoughts and behaviours objectively. My mission with this book is to help deepen your self-awareness, so that you can make conscious choices about how you think and behave as a leader. As you do this, you'll learn that some of these thoughts and behaviours are undoubtedly helpful and contribute to your success, while others are getting in the way of your leadership – either by creating internal noise or having a negative impact on others.

An additional disclaimer: these patterns are not diagnoses, judgements or life sentences! I offer these not as exhaustive descriptions or boxes for everyone to fit into neatly. I'm not offering them as psychometrically valid tools. I share these with you as guidelines and mirrors, so that you are able to recognise certain similarities in yourself (or in those around you!). You may also find a combination across all three that apply to you at different times and in different situations. My belief is that there's a little bit of each of these patterns in all of us. By sharing these patterns and guiding your self-reflection, I want you to be able to recognise what is working for you and what might need to change, so that you can make those conscious choices and ultimately get out of your own way. I want you to unlock your leadership!

So, let's uncover what each of them holds.

GOING FAST

When you are Going Fast as a leader, you are experiencing noise and chaos in your mind. It's a pretty hectic and stressful state to be in. You aren't always stopping to consider the impact you're having as a leader; instead, you find yourself pushing onwards constantly without much clarity around your goals or intentions. Going Fast is typically rushing through daily life, juggling the many commitments and demands that most of us have. But it's also Going Fast in your head: trying to keep up with the cognitive load of solving complex issues, remembering information and working through a long mental to-do list.

To yourself and others, Going Fast might look and feel a little like the checklist on the next page.

Going Fast: what does it look like?

Behaviours *(what others see)*	• Your work calendar is jammed solid • You start the day by diving into the first task/meeting in front of you • Not slowing down to ask questions • Distracted in meetings and conversations • Just-in-time planning or actions
Thoughts *(your inner voice)*	• 'My diary is a nightmare' • 'I don't feel prepared for this conversation' • 'What's going on?' • 'I'm overwhelmed. I can't get on top of this' • 'I'm not sure what's most important here' • 'I don't know what I'm trying to achieve'
Priorities *(your focus)*	• More operational, less strategic • Get shit done • Clear the to-do list as quickly as possible

The importance of noticing

With the volume of information you're exposed to as a busy leader, it's difficult for your brain to focus on any more than the immediate activity in any given moment. Many leaders I speak with complain about this experience as having too many metaphorical tabs open in their brain at once. It's not only exhausting operating this way, it's ineffective. You end up running around, putting out spot fires and chasing rabbits down holes, while feeling like you're not making good progress and with no clear end game in mind. When you're going so fast at work that you rush from meeting to meeting and task to task, it becomes virtually impossible for you to consider and set intentions about how you want to lead.

Max Bazerman is an expert of applied behavioural psychology, Harvard Business School professor, co-director of the Harvard Kennedy School Center for Public Leadership and author of *The Power of Noticing*. Based on three decades of research, his book points out that leaders have to notice and act on information that may not be immediately obvious in order to make better-quality decisions. He describes a state called 'inattentional bias' in which we tend to ignore information that is right in front of us or readily available, even when it is valuable for us to pay attention to it, because we are so caught up in what we are doing or thinking about in that moment. In decision-making terms, by Going Fast we're cutting ourselves off at the knees.

Reframing productivity

I've seen many leaders become almost ninja-like in their ability to run at pace – attending back-to-back meetings, making decisions on the fly because that's what's being demanded, prioritising the urgent over the important because there's seemingly never enough time for the latter. This mode of operating may work for a while, in terms of getting shit done. But I argue we really need to reframe what we mean by being 'productive'! As busy leaders with loads of demands, this way of operating isn't sustainable in the long term.

In contrast, by overcoming this barrier you will know clearly what is most important, what your goals are as a leader and what outcomes you're trying to achieve. These will be consistently present in your mind, allowing you to make better choices and achieve better outcomes. You have to define your intentions first and then do the hard work of ensuring that you're creating space, accessing the right information and operating with awareness as you go forward. Otherwise, you'll be constantly improvising until all of a sudden it all comes out from underneath you and you don't know what to do next. In essence, I'm arguing that in order to go fast, you must first go slow. We'll get into this pattern in more detail in Chapter Five, including how to overcome this way of operating, by *acting with intent*.

HOLDING BACK

When you are Holding Back as a leader, you may find yourself feeling stuck in uncertainty, questioning your abilities or not fully owning your voice. I'm not talking about straightforward introversion; I'm describing a hesitation in making decisions, speaking up and contributing your point of view. It's a stressful, gripping feeling that prevents you from fully stepping into your leadership. The internal barriers that can lead to this include self-doubt, imposter syndrome and being faced with uncertainty (which, let's be honest, is pretty much a constant reality for us all!).

To yourself and others, Holding Back might look and feel a little like the checklist opposite.

Holding Back: what does it look like?

Behaviours *(what others see)*	• Not proactively sharing your view • Putting off making difficult or complex decisions • Body language that seems hesitant or unsure • Couching your views/decisions with caveats: 'I might be wrong, but …' • Seeking more information/assurance before taking action • Asking for validation from others
Thoughts *(your inner voice)*	• 'I don't feel confident to speak up here' • 'I don't know the right answer to this issue' • 'Others have the answers/more to contribute' • 'I can't make this decision yet' • 'Am I really up to this role/task?' • 'I'm not sure leadership/this role is for me'
Priorities *(your focus)*	• Avoiding risk • Securing others' approval or reassurance • Being in a comfort zone • 'Choosing your battles' (very selectively!)

When you hold back, you're undervaluing yourself. You are missing opportunities to provide your unique perspective and show people how much you have to contribute as a leader. Your behaviour might also be presumed as a bit passive aggressive if you withhold from those around you. And there's the risk of creating obstruction for others when you hold back or delay making decisions – as leaders, we have to be decisive, even in situations where we might find it difficult to be so.

CASE STUDY: Michelle is dealing with uncertainty

During the peak of COVID-19, I was speaking with Michelle, who was recently promoted to be CEO of a successful and fast-growing design company. Despite having been an internal successor with many years of experience and great relationships with her colleagues, Michelle found herself in a bewildering situation. Not only was she taking on the role of CEO for the first time, but was also having to navigate some difficult decisions when suddenly faced with the pandemic. The combination of uncertainty, significant pressure from the board and her own questioning of herself in those early days as a first-time CEO made it difficult for her to make quick and confident decisions.

As a result, early in the pandemic Michelle held back. She deferred making some judgement calls on financial issues such as whether to stand down staff and force annual leave, or continue paying her staff while revenues were taking a significant hit. In the board's view, she was taking longer than was necessary to make the call – and it was out of fear of making wrong decisions so early in her tenure.

Eventually, she had a conversation with the company's founder who raised his concerns. After talking it through, Michelle realised that she had to overcome this hesitation in order to give her team the clarity they needed from her. She saw that in this moment of crisis, making a partly informed decision was better than making no decision at all.

Within a matter of days, she decided to allow her staff to keep their roles with a temporary salary reduction. By making her decision transparent and understood, she also reduced uncertainty to some extent for others in the business – which had a massive positive impact on their stress levels and productivity.

Choosing your response

External situations can contribute to you Holding Back, such as being in a toxic work environment, taking on a challenging new role or being told by others (rightly or otherwise) that you lack experience or knowledge. As we explored in Chapter Two, external barriers will always exist; it is your interpretation of those situations and how you choose to respond that makes all the difference to your leadership. You can either choose to hold back, or not.

You might say, 'Surely I don't have to contribute all the time just for the sake of it'. Spot on. There are times when you genuinely won't have the knowledge or value needed to contribute at that moment. I'm not saying that you should be contributing incessantly. This is about course-correcting – getting the balance right between listening and allowing other people space to contribute while still being prepared to add your own voice too.

It's also about the balance of gathering enough information and building surety of your perspective, while continuing to make decisions at pace; knowing that you probably won't ever have the ideal amount of information available to you. Sometimes Holding Back can be an effective move as it allows others space to contribute. It provides you with more information and time to formulate your opinion. Like everything, it's a matter of balance.

When you overcome the pattern of Holding Back, you develop the quiet but steadfast confidence in knowing when and how to contribute your voice. You also understand that you can and should make decisions in spite of uncertainty, with clear strategies and frameworks in mind to help you do this in an effective way. In Chapter Six we delve more deeply into the patterns of Holding Back and highlight the strategies that will help you move towards *having an impact*.

OVERDOING

When you are Overdoing, you are stuck in the trap of perfectionism and caught up in the illusion of control. Overdoing is when you work incredibly hard to ensure your work always hits the mark, eliminating any potential margin of error – but in doing so you inadvertently create problems for yourself and others. You begin thinking that you alone need to fix the problems that others bring to you at work. You also feel a strong sense of needing to be across everything that is happening so that you can try to control situations or prevent things from going wrong.

To yourself and others, Overdoing might look and feel a little like the checklist opposite.

Overdoing: what does it look like?

Behaviours *(what others see)*	• Working more hours than necessary • Being very involved in the detail • Producing all work to an equally high standard • Difficulty prioritising • Significant time reviewing/correcting others' work • Retaining tight control of others' work • Giving people the answers – 'telling' them how to fix problems
Thoughts *(your inner voice)*	• 'I don't think this is good enough' • 'We can't let that happen' • 'It's easier to do it myself' • 'What will others think when they see this?' • 'What if I/we/they mess up?' • 'I have to solve this' • 'I feel like I'm caught up in the weeds'
Priorities *(your focus)*	• Recognition for great outcomes • High standards are maintained • Doing what it takes to avoid mistakes/failures

Pushing to the edge

The harder you strive to achieve an unrealistic standard for yourself or others, the quicker you are putting yourself on the path of burnout. Having high standards probably helped you achieve the success you've had to date. At the same time, you probably also understand logically that you can't possibly work 100 hours every week or be across every single detail of what's happening around you. Operating in this way also makes it hard for other people to be at their best, because you aren't giving them the trust and space to do their jobs the best way they can. When you assume (wrongly) that it is your role as leader to solve every issue for your people, you're robbing them of opportunities to make mistakes and learn in the process. Making mistakes is a valuable opportunity for all of us to grow.

CASE STUDY: James is trapped in Overdoing

James was a successful technical manager who had worked in his field of engineering for 15 years. I met him to debrief a set of psychometric assessments as part of a leadership conference, and we uncovered a range of insights about his individual behaviours and leadership styles. Through that process, James observed that one of his greatest strengths was something that had contributed significantly to his success to date: his determination to produce work of an exceptional quality that would always impress those more senior in the organisation.

Recently appointed to a leadership role managing a large team for the first time, James admitted he had found himself regularly working longer hours than usual. He explained the pressure he felt to ensure he was up-to-date with what each of his team members were doing on a daily basis, resulting in him sitting in on more and more meetings and having multiple one-on-ones throughout each week. He was also doing countless extra hours of work on nights and weekends to review (and 'correct') the output of his team to the standard that he wanted to see.

I asked about the impact this was having on him. James cringed a bit and hesitated. He admitted this workload was adding stress to his family life, as well as some negative effects on his health – crappy sleep and regular headaches.

For the first time, working harder and putting in more hours was not getting James the outcomes he wanted. It was also coming at a real cost to himself and others. Not only was he making his own workload unsustainable, but his direct reports were becoming increasingly frustrated and losing confidence in their ability to meet James' expectations. They felt a distinct lack of autonomy. In the end, James lost several highly talented people in his team and almost reached the point of burnout himself before ultimately deciding to leave the role, as he found the stress and the work levels unmanageable.

Striving for perfection served James' career well to a point ... until he was asked to lead a large team of experienced people who should have been doing most of the detailed work under his broader guidance and with his encouragement.

The trap of Overdoing is not just about having high standards in general (which is obviously a good thing!). It is failing to ensure those standards are realistic, and able to be achieved through others.

INSIGHT COMES FIRST

Being able to recognise one or a combination of these patterns in yourself is the first step to building insight, before finding ways to overcome the patterns that are getting in your way. Holding up that mirror allows you to start pinpointing where some of these patterns may exist for you, so that you can make a conscious choice as to what (if anything) you want to do about them.

David B Peterson is a psychologist, a pioneer in the field of executive coaching, and was formerly the senior director of executive coaching and leadership at Google, Inc. In the best-selling book he co-authored with Mary Dee Hicks, *Development First: Strategies for Self-Development*, Peterson described a concept called the development pipeline – a framework for describing five conditions for sustaining behaviour change. The five conditions start with the first critical step of *insight*. This suggests we must be aware of what is working for us or against us and what we want to achieve before we're in a position to change any behaviour patterns over time.

It's a bit like being sent off for training without any understanding as to why you've been sent. Imagine if your manager signed up your whole team to participate in a training session on presentation skills. It would be easy enough for you to go along, sit in on the course, listen to the expert and write down some notes. However, if you have no idea why you're there in the first place – no understanding of your current speaking skills or whether you need to speak louder, more concisely or with greater passion – then how will you know what you're meant to pay attention to and do differently? Insight is the first step in meaningful development.

It is partly the purpose of this book to help you gain this valuable insight about yourself. But … insight is not the whole story. Insight does not equal motivation to do anything about the issue you are now aware of. Just because you become aware, doesn't mean that you also know what to do differently. This motivation only comes when you consider the impact of this pattern on yourself, your work outcomes and the people around you. Then you can focus on how you want it to be different in future.

 UNLOCKED TIPS

Now that I've outlined the three patterns at a high level and explained the importance of insight, I invite you to really think about how these patterns might relate to you, too. Here are some steps you can take:

- Complete the self-assessments for each of these patterns. As you reflect on each item in the checklists, think about whether it applies to you currently, or perhaps in the past. Has it been a consistent pattern over time?

- Does one pattern (Going Fast, Holding Back or Overdoing) seem to resonate most for you right now? If so, which one?

- How is this pattern actually *helping* you or others? For example, if it is Holding Back, maybe your behaviour ensures others have ample opportunity to contribute. If it's Overdoing, perhaps your behaviour is resulting in really good-quality/low-error work.

- Are there any ways this pattern is creating *problems* for you or others?

- Do you feel like you're a mix of all three patterns? In this case, your current thought and behaviour patterns may be more situational. For example, perhaps at home, you find yourself in Overdoing mode. At work, maybe you've recently taken on a new role and feel like you are in Holding Back mode. Or maybe your workload is especially crazy right now and you find yourself in Going Fast mode. That's completely fine. My suggestion is to pick out one or two key behaviours that you think are most important to focus on, either because they're creating the most problems for you, or because success in your role depends on you shifting this pattern.

- If you are finding it hard to be objective when completing the self-assessments, or you feel like you're not quite seeing yourself in the descriptors, ask an honest friend or family member to sense check with you. Say, 'Hey, I see these two. What do you see?' Otherwise, make a note of them for now and gently observe yourself in action for the next week or two. Which of the dimensions do you start to observe in yourself? Come back after two weeks and complete the assessments again. This may help you to become more aware of thoughts or behaviours that you didn't notice before.

I'M WITH YOU EVERY STEP

You are fluid, dynamic, full of potential and a continuous work in progress. I created this book to be a companion to you – a source of ongoing coaching support. With this book, you will define the leader you want to be, and learn how to gradually overcome any barriers. It's not about eliminating the core parts of who you are. It's about building consistent awareness as a leader, so that you can continue to grow and course-correct as and when you need to. On this journey, there is a good chance that you might find yourself taking a step forward, sideways and perhaps backwards again. That's okay. When you do, you can come back to this book again. Chapter Eight will delve into how you can tackle this challenge of ongoing change and growth.

You are fluid, dynamic, full of potential and a continuous work in progress.

In summing up, there are some common patterns to how leaders think and behave that can get in the way of their effectiveness. You are not alone in experiencing these, and you're not 'broken'! Understanding the pattern that resonates the most for you is the first step towards being able to do something about it. Start reflecting on where your greatest opportunity is right now for your development as a leader. What is your motivation for change?

The rest of the book is focused on what to do differently. Chapters Five to Seven are written to help you more deeply understand each of the three patterns, and provide you with a practical toolkit for operating differently. Chapter Eight is about how to create new patterns over time so you can unlock your potential in a consistent and sustainable way. But first, we'll start with Chapter Five: what to do when you are Going Fast.

CHAPTER FIVE

From Going Fast to Leading With Intent

No one wants to feel like they're on the hamster wheel – spinning around, pouring sweat, near panic, hoping desperately they're moving towards something of value. The most powerful tool I've discovered to get out of this mode is leading with intent. When you lead with intent, you become more influential and less reactive as a leader. Intent is about setting a clear outcome that you hope to achieve as a leader. The outcome could include things like:

- a strategic goal over months or even years of work
- the outcome of a key stakeholder meeting or negotiation
- how another person thinks and feels after interacting with you.

Leading with intent requires you to stop for a minute and determine what outcome you hope to achieve. As suggested above, this could be a tangible result – for example, winning a new client – or an intangible result – for example, how you've made other people think or feel as a result of your leadership. Setting intentions is an important step to help you overcome Going Fast. But this chapter will also guide you to consider a second factor: that is, to consider whether your behaviours are consistent with your intentions. It is important to gather feedback and perspectives from those around you so you can regularly check for this.

Intentions are different to achievements. Intentions allow space for the fact that the actual outcome may not eventuate exactly as you plan, despite your best efforts. There are other forces at play – those forces mainly being other people. But we can and should set intentions as leaders, even if we may not necessarily attain them all the time. Ideally, we should aim for the constructive zone in between two extremes:

1. being so determined and single-minded that we strive to achieve an outcome at all costs

2. bouncing from meeting to meeting, conversation to conversation, working really hard but not being clear about the outcome that we are aiming for or why that outcome is important.

The key to getting off that hamster wheel is making a commitment to stop being reactive so you can amplify your influence as a leader. Day to day, you'll feel more energised and motivated because you'll know what you're aiming to achieve and why. You'll be able to direct your finite energy towards the outcomes you most want to achieve. Leading with intent is more sustainable than Going Fast, and it helps you to avoid burnout.

My recommended four steps to leading with intent are:

1. Discover your intrinsic motivators.
2. Set your intentions.
3. Ask for and listen to feedback.
4. Regularly reflect on whether your actions are aligned with your intent.

I use this approach regularly with my coaching clients. Over and over, they find it incredibly valuable to pause, take a step back from the noise of their busy world and consider what is most important to their leadership. They use this as a way of setting their compass and calibrating their actions accordingly.

Knowing there are consistent steps you can take to help you set, check and reflect on your intentions is a powerful way to help you overcome the barrier of Going Fast. It offers a plan to come back to when you need a reminder – so if you forget, you can always come straight back to this chapter.

CASE STUDY: Cassie reflects on her priorities

Early in 2022 I met Cassie, who was struggling to keep up with the ongoing challenges stemming from the COVID pandemic. I asked her to describe a typical week in her role as a community engagement manager for the local council. She sighed and described in vivid detail what it looked like at the moment: meeting to meeting, back-to-back, week after week – with barely time to look at the agenda for two minutes before the next meeting hit her. She was cramming her 'real work' in after hours, which cut into her personal time and was resulting in many late nights. When I asked her what this frenetic work was like for her, she described it as exhausting, depleting and stressful. She wasn't clear about what she was aiming for, what she was trying to achieve or how she was being perceived among all of this busyness.

After she took some much-needed leave to recharge, and following some positive conversations with a trusted mentor, Cassie was able to step back just long enough to reflect on some important questions:

1. What outcomes do I need to achieve in my role?
2. What impact do I want to have on those around me?

While Cassie was still caught up in crazy amounts of meetings even after this period of reflection, having this opportunity to refocus allowed her to approach her work differently. She noticed she had a more positive sense of direction that sustained her and guided the approach she took into every conversation at work. She turned the answers to these two important questions into two sticky notes and sat them on her computer screen as a visual reminder of her intentions before every meeting, every phone call and every email she sent. She moved forward with clarity on what was most important, in spite of all the noise and ongoing demands around her.

Almost everyone I know is at a similar frenetic level of busyness and therefore stands to gain from pausing to think about their intention. This chapter aims to support you by helping you to think about what is most important to you as a leader and why (this can be described as your intrinsic motivators). I will guide you on how to set those intentions around creating positive change, and the importance of gathering feedback and perspective from others so you can regularly and objectively assess whether your actions are aligned with your intentions.

WHAT REALLY MATTERS TO YOU?

Taking time to discover your intrinsic motivators will allow you to live and lead in a way that is more sustainable for you and, ultimately, more satisfying. Intrinsic motivators are distinct from extrinsic motivators – the latter being the 'rewards' people go after in their careers such as money, promotions, material possessions, awards, recognition and profile or status. These are not inherently bad; we all need to pay the bills and enjoy a hard-won accolade now and again. However, it is the *intrinsic* motivators – those inner rewards, the feeling of satisfaction – that will sustain us in a meaningful way throughout our careers.

If you need convincing here, I want you to think about a time when someone gave you an award at school or work. It probably felt good to receive it, right? But compare this to an experience you've had of working really hard to achieve something you really cared about – like training for a marathon to help raise funds for a charity, even though you weren't a strong runner.

A personal example for me was having the guts to write this book. The hard slog, sleep deprivation and anxiety of writing wasn't fuelled by wanting to sell a stack of books – that would have been an extrinsic motivator. I was fuelled by wanting the experience of creating a book and the chance to share my perspective with as many people as could hopefully benefit. These intrinsic motivators were the things that kept me going.

Tapping into your intrinsic motivations as a leader means you're able to find a sense of meaning in your work, despite the many challenges you may face. They can guide you to become clear on your intentions. Perhaps they will allow you to feel a sense of joy and satisfaction from your work as a leader – although we can all safely admit this might feel like a stretch on some days!

One of my favourite books of all time is *Drive: The Surprising Truth About What Motivates Us*, written by Dan Pink – a well-known social psychologist and leading expert in human motivation. The book describes research showing that extrinsic motivators are effective when it comes to transactional work – for example, answering phone calls on high volume in a call centre. However, they have the opposite effect when it comes to discretionary or creative effort, like solving problems in the workplace or coming up with new ideas and plans. It's this discretionary effort that relates to the majority of our work as leaders. Our intrinsic motivators are key to unlocking human motivation for difficult tasks, and the same goes for leadership. Leadership can be bloody hard work, so we all need reminding at the end of the day what we're doing this for.

In *Drive*, Pink explains self-determination theory (originally developed by psychologists Richard Ryan and Edward Deci), which describes three concepts – relatedness, autonomy and competence – as our basic psychological needs. We can draw on our intrinsic motivators when we pursue the work of leadership because it offers us a chance to hold independence (autonomy), be part of something bigger than ourselves (relatedness) and get better in our role as leaders (competence).

I've lost count of the number of leaders who have admitted to me that they sometimes don't like or agree with what they've been asked to do, and therefore find it very difficult to experience internal satisfaction as a result. If this is true for you, reframe the way you're thinking about your work. For example, rather than focus on the tasks you dislike or how unpleasant it is for you: focus instead on the autonomy, relatedness or competence aspects of your work. For example, rather than doing the task alone, could you do the task with others, to be part of something bigger than yourself? Could you see the task as an opportunity to get better and develop your skills? The key here is to dig deep to find a gem of motivation within a difficult situation.

To be clear – there is absolutely nothing wrong in itself with wanting to earn money or be promoted. But the point is that those things alone won't sustain you for a whole career, or through the ups and downs of leadership. Extrinsic motivators (like being given a big bonus) are like having a massive hit of sugar: it feels great for a quick moment but it doesn't sustain you. You only end up craving more. I've seen many leaders who have relentlessly pursued promotion after promotion, almost for the sake of progression alone, only to reach a point where they felt completely lost in terms of their work's purpose. They ultimately lose sight of what they want their career and work to be about.

In March 2022, Ash Barty, the former world number one tennis player, shocked the sporting world and the Australian public with her retirement announcement. She was quoted at the time as saying that she left feeling proud and fulfilled. In contrast, I considered at that moment other elite athletes who continue to stay on in their sport, even after achieving many goals. I couldn't help but wonder, given everything these athletes had already achieved, what else could they be pursuing? Perhaps more money, more world records and more endorsements? Maybe a bigger legacy or profile for themselves? Again, there's nothing wrong with this as such, but it struck me how differently Barty must have viewed her own version of achievement and satisfaction, compared perhaps to other athletes who were still – apparently – chasing *something*.

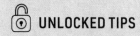 **UNLOCKED TIPS**

At this point, I want you to reflect on what is most important to you in your leadership and why. In your role as a leader:

- What outcome do you most want to achieve?
  - For example, *I want my team to be known as high achieving*, or *I want to create a positive workplace culture in this function.*

- Why is this important to you?
  - For example, *I want my team to feel a sense of pride in their work*, or *I believe everyone in this function deserves to be treated with respect and fairness.*

- What gives you the greatest satisfaction in your work?
  - For example, *seeing my team achieve their goals and grow their careers.*

- What is one positive change you want to influence?
  - For example, *helping my team see the value of collaboration*, or *influencing our executives to understand the importance of diversity.*

Write down answers to each of these and then test them out with someone you trust. When you say them out loud, do they sound truthful to you? What feedback did you get from the person you shared them with?

Other people's yardsticks for how they define 'success' do not necessarily have to align with your own (while noting you still need to deliver on the stated performance objectives of your role, of course!). This is about defining your story, identifying your intrinsic motivators and determining what is valuable to you alone. Your purpose as a leader is not for others to determine.

SETTING YOUR INTENTIONS

As distinct from thinking about your purpose and overall goals as a leader, setting intentions – as we touched on in Chapter Three – helps determine your focus in the short term. Setting intentions regularly about how you want to lead and the impact you want to have is also the best way to move out of reactive mode and create positive change around you. Change, as we all know, doesn't happen accidentally. Whether it's a change in career, developing a new skill, strengthening a relationship with a stakeholder, building a positive culture in your team or turning around the performance of a business, it takes that first seed of an idea which grows into an intention and then into a series of actions. This section is about helping you set clear intentions that:

- you can stick to
- motivate you
- have a positive benefit for you and others.

Your intention should be a statement that describes what you intend to do or how you intend to be as a leader, including the tangible outcomes and felt impact you want to have on others. An example of a tangible outcome is intending to restructure your team so it is more aligned with the future direction of the business. An example of the felt impact you want to have is making your team feel inspired to learn and try new things. The latter in particular is not about achieving a KPI. It's about having a positive influence on the people you are leading.

Your intention should be set with a short-term focus, based on your goals, values and the current situations you face. So, try to focus on what will make the biggest positive difference to you and others over a specific period of time. For example, you might say to yourself, 'During my meetings over the next fortnight, I intend to ...':

- ask for and give lots of feedback
- be calm
- be focused on my main priority
- share my perspective more
- listen and be more fully present.

When you get in the habit of setting and reflecting on intentions, it's important to note these will evolve and change as you try different things and receive more feedback ... and that is completely okay.

Bottom line: we all want to know that our hard work and effort is going to pay off. Our subconscious mind is capable of doing some very clever cost-benefit analyses about whether an action or effort is *really* worth our while. By self-determining what is most important for you to achieve (rather than using a generic external standard of success), you're able to have a clear set of intentions to keep you going and guide your actions.

CASE STUDY: Mark finds a way to refocus

A senior supply chain manager in the FMCG industry, Mark was working at a frenetic pace throughout COVID-19. His role required him to be on hand almost around the clock to respond to queries and provide support to his clients.

He told me during this period that he was moving so fast it felt like he was 'throwing paint at a wall and hoping that something would stick', every day. Mark knew his clients were generally experiencing frustration and uncertainty. Yet despite his many years of experience, he didn't know if any of his hard efforts to address these concerns were actually making a difference.

When I asked him, he couldn't articulate what difference he was hoping to make or the outcome he was trying to achieve. He was, in reality, just trying to keep his head above water. The solution was to step back and work out what he really needed to focus on. He spent some time proactively connecting with his clients, getting a feel for their issues and hearing their concerns firsthand. He realised the thing he most wanted to do in his role was to amplify his clients' voices to be heard at the executive level of his organisation. Mark recognised through this reflection that he wanted to be an advocate for his clients, because he believed they deserved better.

He found this intention by defining the positive change he wanted to see as a result of his work as a leader. His intention was about wanting to see the clients and their needs at the centre of all the products and services his organisation provided. Once he set this intention, Mark could start to focus his actions and his behaviour. He noticed feeling more energy day to day. He also started to speak up more with his boss about the issues his clients were experiencing. This was a powerful result from setting his intention and understanding what was important to him and why.

Let's be clear – intention alone won't get the job done. Positive change also takes action, decisions, collective effort, skills, resources and persistence. However, intention is the spark and the compass. It sets you on your way. It is the first and most important ingredient you need to achieve great outcomes.

 UNLOCKED TIPS

Building on your reflection in Chapter Three, take a few minutes now to come up with one leadership intention that will make the biggest positive difference to you and others over the coming week. Once you have taken a moment to set that intention:

- Take a photo of it with your phone, set a recurring reminder in your calendar, or write it down on a sticky note and put it in a place that you'll see regularly.

- For one week, look at that note at the beginning of every work day and just before each meeting you have that day.

By setting these intentions and keeping them in the foreground of your thinking, you are much more likely to take action and behave in alignment with those intentions.

A word of warning: something that may distract you or get in your way here is listening too much to other people's ideas of what you should be doing, and not enough to what you see as most important. Your employer may set your KPIs, but remember that people will ultimately remember you for the type of leader you are. This is something that is really up to you to define and work towards.

STOP TO CHECK

It's one thing to start with your intentions, but real leadership impact comes when you regularly stop to check that your behaviour is consistent with those intentions. You can check by asking for and listening to honest feedback that helps overcome any blind spots. Once you've set your intentions, they provide you with a 'target destination' – a point of reference that allows you to check regularly if your *intended* way of leading and your *actual* way of leading have a good amount of overlap. It's like setting the GPS in your car's sat nav and then occasionally looking down at the navigation to make sure you're still heading in the right direction. When you've done the great work of thinking about your motivators and the impact you want to have as a leader, it's worth spending a bit of time and effort making sure you are on track with that intention. In addition to personal reflection, the best way to do this is to seek feedback from those around you, using the unlocked tips I shared earlier in Chapter Three.

SLOWING DOWN TO GO FAST

If you feel like all of this might take too much time or effort and you just want to get on with the task at hand, remember: this is about helping you to slow down in order to go fast. It will help you to achieve your leadership goals much quicker in the end.

Now that you are nearing the end of this chapter, take 10 minutes right now to answer these questions as a summary of all the work you've done so far:

- *What are your intrinsic motivators?* What matters most to you as a leader and why? What do you find most fulfilling about your work?

- *What are your intentions as a leader?* What impact do you most want to have on others?

Make sure you write the answers down on those sticky notes and then put them in your preferred highly visible spot. Some of the best places I've heard used include a laptop screen, hallway mirror, car dashboard, inside your wallet or even on the back of the toilet door (there's some good thinking time available there!).

As I suggested earlier, read your responses each morning, before each meeting and even again at the end of the day to help you evaluate. Even on the busiest days when you are in back-to-back meetings, I encourage you to take micro breaks of one minute and take three or four slow, deep breaths. These deep breaths are a sure-fire strategy to help regulate your autonomic nervous system and re-engage your prefrontal cortex, taking you out of your fight-or-flight threat mode when you're feeling stressed. Once you're in this state, read your intention, or visualise it if it isn't physically with you. If you need to, you may even get it down to one word that helps sum up your intention – for example, *composed, supportive, focused, confident.* This is a great way to easily remind yourself of the impact you want to have on others in the next interaction you have.

In our busy lives it's easy to fall back into the trap of Going Fast, so keep those sticky notes up-to-date and visible. If you find yourself getting sucked back into old habits, find an accountability buddy – someone who is happy to listen to you talk about your progress and give you some honest feedback along the way.

To sustain your leadership efforts and achieve satisfaction and fulfillment in your work, you need to focus on what is important to you intrinsically, and what difference you most want to make as a leader.

Apply the process for setting those intentions and checking in with yourself and others to make sure your behaviour and actions are consistent with those intentions.

I want you to stay off that exhausting hamster wheel, so that others will benefit from experiencing the absolute best version of your leadership.

In the next chapter, we'll look at a different pattern of thinking and behaviour that so often results in genuine angst and lost opportunities for leaders – Holding Back. I describe how it happens and what to do about it.

CHAPTER SIX

From Holding Back to Having an Impact

Leadership asks you to step forward, to form a point of view and express your perspective for many reasons – but in some situations, this can be hard to do. And yet when you hold back due to uncertainty or self-doubt, you are short-changing yourself, your work and the people around you who are counting on your leadership.

When I see leaders Holding Back, it's most often due to two things:

1. *Self-doubt.* Most of us have experienced this at some point. It's a kind of knotted, tense feeling in your stomach and a form of anxiety; a worry about what might come out of your mouth and how it will make you look in others' eyes; or a concern you won't get it 'right'. So you don't speak up. You hold back your point of view.

2. *Uncertainty.* This is the hesitancy and overwhelm that comes when a decision is looming and you don't know the answer. Perhaps you procrastinate and delay making the decision until you can gather more information and seek more clarity. Or you may defer elsewhere by asking someone else to make the decision. This is often directed upwards, which your manager probably won't love because ideally they want you to come to them with solutions, not problems to solve.

It's easy enough to fall into the Holding Back trap in the chaotic and uncertain world we live in. Some typical signals that you are Holding Back include:

- people are harassing you for clarity on what they need to be doing or for you to give them guidance on what's happening
- you're being told (more than once) that you need to speak up and contribute more in team meetings
- you notice that you've left key meetings without contributing, even though you had a definite point of view to share.

The Holding Back pattern describes both a conscious avoidance of taking action (which causes unnecessary delays and bottle-necks) and a subconscious hesitation or doubt (which can create stress and anxiety in you and a huge opportunity cost for others). When you hold back, those around you miss the benefit of your knowledge and your unique perspective as a leader. You also miss the benefit of demonstrating your full value, which can impact how your peers, leaders and other stakeholders then view your capability. Whatever is causing you to hold back, by tackling these internal barriers head-on with courage and determination, you will set yourself up to have a much bigger impact in your leadership role.

CASE STUDY: It's not just you

Several years ago, I was fortunate to work with a group of leaders who were identified as high potential in a global retail organisation. These leaders completed a series of psychometric assessments and sat down one-on-one with me for a conversation about their personality style and their behaviours in the workplace. During the program, we discussed a lot of ideas in relation to influencing skills. As part of the coaching discussions on that topic, I heard every single participant – all 20 of them – describe situations over the previous months where they had felt that they had 'held back'. For example, they attended a project meeting in which they weren't sure if they should speak up, or they were asked to make a key decision and deferred to others' opinions instead of making it themselves.

When we explored the underlying story in this group of experienced, clever and committed leaders, I heard many of the same concerns expressed. These included:

- 'I don't know enough about this topic to add anything of value.'
- 'What if I've got it wrong?'
- 'There are too many other, louder voices around me in this meeting.'
- 'I don't have enough information to make this decision.'

I've heard many hundreds of similar concerns expressed since, by leaders in a range of settings and stages of career. It's a timely reminder that, if you sometimes experience these thoughts, it's not just you.

This chapter empathises with every reader who has felt a version of this hesitation, self-doubt or uncertainty. I want you to know that this also includes me! I have historically been a master of Holding Back. It has been my default way of operating whenever I am out of my comfort zone, doing something new in an environment where I don't know how others view me, or when I have to make decisions and do work with a lot of uncertainty around it. I'm making progress, but it never fully retreats. So if you see yourself reflected in this pattern, I completely get it. This chapter puts a spotlight on the two most common ways you may be Holding Back and encourages you to reframe your thinking so you can conquer that hesitation when you need to.

OVERCOMING UNCERTAINTY

You can make decisions and take action as a leader despite uncertainty. Uncertainty is an unavoidable constant in all of our lives in this fast-changing world. In the work you do, you'll face it in never-ending ways. What will my customers or clients want next month? What will my competitors be doing next year? Who will my competitors even be? Will my employees be ready to meet the challenges that we will face? How will technology change the way I'm doing business? What will be going on in the world in general?

For leaders, it's a constant challenge to counter this reality of uncertainty with the ability to make decisions and avoid inertia for themselves, their teams and their organisation. As the old saying goes, making a bad decision is better than making no decision at all. Freezing – Holding Back from making a decision or taking action due to uncertainty or lack of information – can stifle activity in a business and create frustration for others who are looking to you to make a call (no pressure!).

There is a key difference between Holding Back – which I consider to be a barrier – and an appropriate level of listening or gathering more information before making a decision – which I think is constructive. But how do you know the difference between constructively listening or Holding Back for too long? In reality, most leaders say they never have the ideal amount of information, particularly when it comes to big, high-stakes decisions. To avoid Holding Back, you will learn to get the timing right between gathering more information and having to make the call.

It's also about overcoming this discomfort by knowing you can only ever make the best decision based on the information that's available to you. The fear of getting it wrong is the source of this anxiety. It might be helpful to consider a worst-case scenario. Rarely is making a wrong call in business a matter of life or death. Decisions aren't about always getting the right answer, but can also be a valuable opportunity to learn. We will look at this further in the next chapter. Even for those decisions that are truly high-stakes– such as those made by doctors, engineers or in the defence forces – rarely will that leader have all the ideal information, complete certainty or a playbook that's going to guide them in all instances and scenarios.

Think about Chesley 'Sully' Sullenberger, the pilot who was forced to make an emergency landing of a plane in New York's Hudson River in 2009. He certainly wasn't in a situation where he had all the information he would ideally want. We all have to contend with needing to take action despite uncertainty, based on the experience we have and the information available to us at the time. This is not about jumping in and making high-stakes decisions without taking at least some degree of due diligence. But it's also not about Holding Back out of fear or uncertainty when others are relying on you to make a call. People need to feel confident in their leader and want direction and clarity, especially in difficult times – these are the times when being authoritative is what counts.

 UNLOCKED TIPS

Paul Saffo is a Silicon Valley–based technology forecaster and consulting professor at Stanford University. He describes a powerful technique I often share with leaders to help them overcome their uncertainty, called 'strong opinions, weakly held'. This framework enables you to make decisions or 'forecasts' with incomplete information, thereby overcoming the freeze effect of Holding Back that I've described in this chapter. The key steps involved in this process are:

1. Form a tentative hypothesis on the given situation. Use your instinct if you must. This is the 'strong opinion' part.

2. Gather information to either confirm or even (ideally) counter your hypothesis. Saffo calls this 'engaging in creative doubt'.

3. Be prepared to revise your hypothesis or your decision – that is, change your mind based on the information you receive from this point forward, or as the scenario unfolds. This is the 'weakly held' part of the equation.

You may find yourself feeling uncomfortable with the idea of overtly gathering information that will challenge your 'strong opinion'. The key with this process is to remember that wisdom sits in distancing yourself from your ideas. You are not your opinions. Part of your role as a leader is that you can – and should – seek to challenge your own views. This process gives you space to change your opinions and be disproven, while still knowing that you inherently have value as a leader. Your role is to help others and your organisation continue moving forward.

WORRY, WORRY, WORRY

We need leaders to have empathy for other people. Empathy (as part of emotional intelligence) can be learned, but many people have a natural tendency to possess and show empathy that is cognitive ('I understand your situation'), emotional ('I empathise with how you are feeling') and behavioural ('I will take action that reflects my empathy'). For those leaders who know they have pronounced sensitivity or empathy for others, I want you to know this is a powerful leadership strength that is sorely needed in the world of work. At times, though, I've also seen it become a contributing factor in Holding Back.

Empathy and sensitivity to others allows leaders to notice when people need them to respond in a certain way. It allows leaders to express understanding for another person's situation or perspective, which then enables the other person to feel understood. These leaders can also demonstrate their consideration by acting on that empathy. However, a strong empathic tendency can at times cause people to hold back from their role as a leader, based on concern for how the action or decision will make another person feel or respond.

Consider the following examples:

- needing to give negative feedback to a team member who is underperforming, but is also going through a rough time in their personal life

- needing to take over a project that was being led by a colleague, knowing how much this may affect their confidence

- needing to call out poor behaviour in a group setting but being worried it might affect the relationships in the group

- needing to make a financial decision in the best commercial interests of the business, knowing it will affect people's roles and careers.

Your empathy for others is a strength to be celebrated and leveraged. But if it is *overplayed*, it may cause you worry that will constrain the role you must adopt as a leader. Your well-tuned empathy can also be stressful in some situations where you are constantly helping or supporting others, leading to what's called compassion fatigue. This is empathising beyond a reasonable point to where you absorb the other person's feelings as your own, or when you can no longer bring yourself to feel compassionate because it's all been a bit too much. Lastly, it's worth considering that you could be taken advantage of by individuals who will use you for your kindness and to avoid being held accountable themselves. In his book *Give and Take,* Adam Grant refers to these as two categories of folks: 'Givers' – those who want to help but can potentially be taken advantage of and manipulated by others – the 'Takers'.

Your empathy for others is a strength to be celebrated and leveraged. But if it is *overplayed*, it may cause you worry that will constrain the role you must adopt as a leader.

Again, and without question, empathy is absolutely an attribute to be encouraged, developed and used as a basis for leadership.

This quality only becomes an issue if it prevents you from being constructive – for example, if it gets in the way of you making a tough decision in a timely way when you need to.

As a healthy balance, by all means feel for the other person while remembering it's not your role to take on the burden of everyone's challenges. As a leader, you don't have to solve everyone's problems. It's important to set boundaries. For instance, do you have a particular relationship that is overly one-sided? Assess how much you're putting in versus what the other person is doing for you. How much time in your discussions seems to be spent on the other person airing their issues and needs versus your own? What proportion of your discussions end up with you or the other person coming away with their needs met? Is it evenly spread?

Also, beware your bias and assumptions. People you like or who are like you may be even harder for you to be firm with. Use your empathy to listen and understand the person, but then make sure you step back to appraise what the situation is objectively and what must happen next from the perspective of the person and your organisation. Some things you could consider saying are, 'Help me understand more,' or 'What I hear you saying is ...' or 'What I am now thinking is ...' or 'Here is what I think could be our next step forward ...'.

Habit might impede you here – these tendencies may be hard-wired into you by function of your personality or your values. Maybe you want to be kind, supportive and empathetic as a leader (and without a doubt we need more leaders like this!). These suggestions aren't intended to devalue or change the positive parts of who you are as a leader. But be aware of when or if any of these tendencies are getting in the way and causing you to hold back.

NOBODY IS A KNOW-IT-ALL

You cannot know everything, but at the same time, you are in your role for a reason. A common cause of Holding Back is concern that the topic being discussed is not your area of expertise, or that you will be shown up as being 'less than others' in terms of your knowledge of the topic.

If you are in your role and included as part of a discussion, whatever it relates to, then there is justification for your contribution. You have knowledge, experience and perspective to offer without needing to necessarily hold a PhD in everything (or anything!). How freeing would it be to know that you don't need to know everything before you understand your value, and therefore know there is value in your perspective?

There is a strong diversity argument here, too. Every organisation I know faces myriad complex problems in need of creative, adaptive solutions. Significant bodies of research and even passed legislation has reaffirmed that organisations need diverse talent to help solve these complex problems – that is, diverse in terms of gender, age, ability, cultural background, work experience, education, geography and so on. The best answer to complex issues is not ever going to be from one person's perspective alone – one presumed expert with all the answers. Hence the value in contributing your perspective as part of that collective view.

You could argue, 'I don't want to speak up for the sake of it, especially if I feel like I'm not necessarily adding any value to a conversation.' If you are only contributing for the sake of it, I would agree! But underestimating the value of sharing your perspective is a huge risk. As I described in Chapter One, when we don't contribute our unique perspectives we not only limit our own potential and how we're perceived by others, we're also missing out on contributing to the vast amounts of collective leadership we need in organisations and our communities to create positive change.

There are some barriers that might impede you acting on this advice. One is the assumption that only having the perfect answer to the issue gives you some golden key or a right to speak up. Remember that your seat at the table is already won. You are in your role for a reason. Also, you can always position your thoughts in those forums as questions or 'I wonder' statements. For example, 'I haven't been in this situation before, and what I'm wondering now is ...' or 'I'm curious about what would happen if ...'. Never underestimate a well-timed and insightful question for opening up possible aspects that have not yet been considered. Remember that fresh perspectives and good inquiry are crucial for deepening discussion and exploring unseen possibilities, especially regarding complex issues.

SPEAKING UP WHEN YOU'RE NOT BEING GIVEN THE MIC

Contributing your voice in a system that is not actively encouraging it takes courage – but it's necessary for strong leadership. You need to use your voice by providing your point of view during discussions, debate and decision-making. But sometimes the system works against you in your attempts to do so.

The visual that always comes to my mind here is an imaginary singer with a fabulous voice that no one's heard yet, standing on a stage in front of a crowd who would all benefit from hearing her sing. The singer is nervous, but knows deep down she wants to share her talents with this crowd. However, when she finally steps forward, the microphone is dangling *just* out of reach. Or being hogged by someone else. Or maybe it's switched off at the power source.

You may be someone who can relate to this. You might be in an industry that's dominated, for example, by one particular gender – be that male or female. You may work in an organisation that values the voices of certain people over others. You may experience exclusion by function of your cultural background, abilities, beliefs, orientation or values in life. You may have been placed in a box by function of others' perspectives of you and your potential. All of these are common experiences of people I work with and can cause you to question yourself and hold back your point of view when you shouldn't. When the system around you makes you feel this way, it can start to erode your own self-worth as a leader. It allows others to determine your value.

Speaking up as a leader is correlated with higher engagement, higher intent to stay with your organisation and higher performance over time. A research study conducted at Microsoft with 6000 managers showed that the more senior leaders were, the more likely they were to be exposed to broader issues and feel more secure in their role, and the more likely they were to contribute their point of view as a result. However, those less senior in the organisation were more likely to only speak on issues that related to their role directly, if indeed at all. The other factors that made the biggest difference to whether someone would speak up included manager behaviour (whether their boss was encouraging) and team climate (whether the team encouraged diverse perspectives).

The latter point on team climate has in recent years become widely promoted as a key issue by Amy Edmondson, professor of leadership at Harvard Business School and a pioneering psychologist in the field of psychological safety. When psychological safety is present in a team environment, it helps encourage those team members to speak up and contribute their point of view.

Leaders have a role in creating the conditions for psychological safety, by actively seeking out, listening to and acting on diverse perspectives of those in their team.

At this point, the last thing I want you to think is that you're expected to change a whole system around you – especially one that you feel might be working against you. It's important, however, to acknowledge these types of external barriers so that you can adopt the best way of thinking about them and therefore find ways to overcome them within your own realm of control. Keep in mind that if your motivation to continue to try is waning, this can further affect your confidence and how you see your own value over time. Plus, by Holding Back you're limiting your opportunities to have the impact that you could have as a leader and to ultimately show others what you have to offer.

 UNLOCKED TIPS

Here are my three tips for finding your voice in this type of environment:

1. Leverage your strengths. Remember the value of your unique view, along with your many other attributes – such as astuteness, empathy, good questioning skills and the transferable skills you bring. Whatever your strengths are, focus on applying those strengths to your given situation. There are lots of assessments available to help you identify your strengths, including the online VIA Character Strengths Survey which is free.

2. Form your point of view on the key issues of the day and articulate them, remembering 'strong opinions, weakly held'.

3. Choose your battles. Some aspects of the system you can influence over time while other parts will likely never change. Develop the astuteness (or wisdom!) to know where and when to exert your energy and attempt to influence change. If you're not sure how to determine where to draw that line, I always say to start with your values and intent (which you can revisit in Chapter Five).

YOUR VOICE IS YOUR IMPACT

You've hopefully reflected through this chapter that your role as a leader requires you to make decisions and contribute your point of view, even when those actions are hard to do. The task now is to stop Holding Back on the basis of fear, uncertainty or self-doubt. Instead, start focusing on the value your perspective can offer the situation and people in front of you – even if it's in the form of a powerful question or hypothesis. Make decisions based on the information available, remembering that you as a person are not your points of view, which are subject to change! Be open to having your ideas and perspectives challenged as information comes to light. This psychological flexibility is a critical skill that will support you as we continue to face complexity and uncertainty in the world around us.

In the next chapter, we'll change gears significantly from Holding Back to Overdoing – a pattern of thinking and especially behaviour that can create significant frustration for others and can seriously get in the way of you unlocking your leadership potential. I'll share ways in which you can overcome this pattern and empower both yourself and those around you in the process.

CHAPTER SEVEN

From Overdoing to Knowing What Counts

Your success as a leader is not dependent on having all the answers, fixing all the problems or being everything to everyone. Rather, successful leadership comes from reframing your role as a leader and resetting your measures of success.

From the beginning of our careers (actually, our whole lives!) it is reinforced to us that it is good to achieve, to get things right and to be the best. However, as you take up the role of leader there is a crucial transition that must occur. That transition is about no longer seeing yourself as the point of focus when it comes to making things happen and achieving great results. Rather, it's seeing yourself as the enabler, with the focus squarely on lifting up everyone around you to achieve success. Without this transition, you risk falling into the pattern of Overdoing.

As a leader, overcoming this pattern is key to:

- helping others grow and achieve success
- finding enduring satisfaction in your own work
- enjoying sustainable performance (and avoiding burnout).

CASE STUDY: Lauren learns to loosen the reins

When I met Lauren she came across as a highly driven and intelligent corporate affairs leader who was looking for better ways to manage her stress and workload. Early in our work together, Lauren described the frustration of the constant rework that she had to do with her team's work, before it was at a point she could send it on to her boss for endorsement. This was creating a lot of additional effort for her, but worse – she was worried that the team had gradually stopped trying and now expected her to do the work for them. When I asked what led to this situation, Lauren explained that the first time a version of work went to her boss without her tight review, her boss was highly critical and told her that the team needed to lift its standards. At that point, Lauren became fearful that her team's work, if less than perfect, would reflect badly on her in her boss's eyes. As a result, she'd been stepping in to prevent that from occurring but, in doing so, had become harsh with her own feedback and prevented her team from owning their work. She was also creating an unsustainable amount of work for herself in the process. Lauren had fallen into one of the most common traps of Overdoing.

Slowly but surely, Lauren started to put in place different ways of working with her team. This included providing more feedback early on, giving them more space to come up with their own solutions and allowing more work to 'pass through' without feeling like she needed to rework every tiny detail.

She was amazed at the difference this made to her capacity, her team's engagement levels and the way it freed her up to focus on other important aspects of her role – such as strategic planning and stakeholder management. She also felt – unsurprisingly – a lot less stressed!

This chapter describes the patterns of Overdoing you may see in others or recognise in yourself. To help you overcome these barriers, I will encourage you to rethink how you define success in your role. I'll also provide you with practical ways to put yourself on a path that frees you from Overdoing – just like Lauren.

THE ANTIHERO MOVEMENT

Your role as a leader is not about being the hero and solving all the problems that are brought your way. This trap is based on the false assumption that you must be 'at the centre' and directly involved in solving the issues your team faces. For centuries, society has put leaders on a pedestal. Famous historical figures, from politicians to religious leaders to activists, have been looked up to, admired and followed by the people around them as well as the generations that followed. Psychologists and philosophers call this 'the great man theory' – the idea that certain individuals have special innate traits that mean they could shape history by function of their superior courage, intellect, leadership prowess and ability to inspire others. The theory suggests these people were 'born with it'. While that theory of leadership has largely been challenged by modern psychological and management research, our subconscious way of thinking about the role of a leader can still be entrenched in the past – namely, that a leader is someone who should ideally have the answers, provide the north star and guide the rest of us mere mortals.

Your role as a leader is not about being the hero and solving all the problems that are brought your way.

The catch here, as I outlined in Chapter One, is that the world is continuing to become more complex. It's becoming less and less plausible that one person alone can solve the many tricky challenges faced by organisations and society at large, regardless of how clever or hardworking that person is. Further, demographic changes mean that younger generations coming into the workplace have different expectations of how they want to be led. They value the opportunity to learn from their leaders and to be provided the chance to learn themselves, as opposed to seeing leaders as the answer to all of their problems and questions. The idea here is to shift towards being an 'antihero' leader – a term described by social entrepreneur and writer Richard Wilson. By embracing this antihero idea of leadership, you can free yourself from an unrealistic and ineffective way of thinking about your role, as well as from an idea that doesn't work in the modern workplace.

YOU CAN'T DO LEADERSHIP ON YOUR OWN

Dr Ronald Heifetz, Marty Linsky and Alexander Grashow introduced the adaptive leadership model in their book *The Practice of Adaptive Leadership: Tools and Tactics for Changing Your Organization and the World*. Put simply, Heifetz, Linsky and Grashow pointed out that the single-figure top-down leadership model is outdated and impractical. As I said before, no single person can solve all of an organisation's problems. This is partly because much of the work of leadership involves needing to influence human behaviour – for example, supporting people to be more customer focused or innovative.

These types of challenges are what Heifetz, Linsky and Grashow call adaptive problems. They can't be solved with a given set of rules, standard protocols or basic regulations. It's not like fixing a machine! Adaptive problems are dynamic and people-centred, hence they require leadership. They are problems that need more than just one person applying their existing know-how and experience to solve. They require leaders who can overcome the very basic human need to feel important and valued and the desire to experience a sense of control. But when we're caught up in Overdoing, we lose sight of this broader perspective and just keep working harder to find those answers and solve those problems.

The pull of leadership responsibility might draw you backwards here. After all, you have no doubt achieved success in your career to date precisely by having lots of answers and doing a great job yourself! So it makes sense that, as a leader now, the expectations seem to be even higher for knowing what to do next. To help you get around this thinking, I want you to remember all the times that *you* had a leader who gave you all the answers, even when you felt you had your own point of view to offer. What did that leader miss out on? What are you missing out on, potentially, if you're trying to solve everything for others?

There are some caveats. In a crisis or an emergency situation some degree of 'command and control' leadership is not only justified but necessary – for example, for those operating under military conditions, or even during peak crisis points in the pandemic.

Under very tight timeframes and with high-stakes situations like these, people really need clarity and one single point of decision-making much more than they need to be involved in solving the problem. Nonetheless, for most of us in leadership roles in day-to-day situations, command and control just won't cut it.

 UNLOCKED TIPS

In his powerful book *Humble Inquiry: The Gentle Art of Asking Instead of Telling*, Edgar Schein writes that the heart of a leader's role is asking, as opposed to telling or directing. The guidance that Schein provides is so helpful for flipping your behaviour from having the answers, to drawing more from others. He suggests:

- Acknowledging your dependence on others. Schein calls this 'here and now humility'. As a leader, others help you identify solutions, solve complex problems and achieve outcomes, and this dependence requires humility. See yourself as just one component of a problem-solving team.

- Explicitly telling people you do not have all the answers, and that you're depending on them to help you solve problems and deliver outcomes. This puts them on notice to contribute! In this process, you want to aim for curiosity over knowing the right answers. Be curious about the ideas that they have, as well as all the possible solutions that perhaps you've not yet considered.

- Seeking others' input in a genuine and authentic way, on the basis that you genuinely believe they have perspectives and contributions you need and that are valuable.

Earlier I described the normal human desire for feeling important and in control. Be sure to watch out for and be prepared to challenge your own sense of ego. It's easy to become seduced by the idea that, as the leader, you alone hold the keys to all of the problems that you and your team face. You might also work in an environment where the idea of a leader as hero is supported. Maybe you have a boss who feels trapped by this themselves or maybe your performance management system reinforces the idea that success equates to you being the one who has all the answers and gets the job done.

If either of these is the case, you're best to pursue adaptive leadership and humble inquiry to help you solve problems. But remember to appropriately claim credit for the outcomes you're able to facilitate with others. A simple but powerful way to do this is to use the term 'I' when pointing to your achievements, in balance with the team's contribution when describing the 'what and how' of those achievements. For example, if your team has just landed a big new client opportunity, you could say something like, 'I've been able to provide guidance to the team on the right strategies for developing new business. With their hard work and persistence, they have been able to secure this new opportunity.'

THE ILLUSION OF CONTROL

When you strive for control, you are chasing an illusion that hampers yourself and others. This is another habit of Overdoing. This trap is based on attempting, in vain, to be across absolutely everything and to try to mitigate anything from going wrong.

If this is you, you are not alone. It makes a lot of sense because we're directly and indirectly taught from an early age that mistakes are bad and should be avoided. Striving for control is a defence mechanism. We're trying to avoid something happening that we assume will be uncomfortable or make us look bad in the eyes of others, or even ourselves.

When I use the word 'control', in practice I mean trying to ensure that you know everything that is happening by carefully tracking how work is being done by others and leaving no room for error in the output that is produced by your team. The vision that always comes to mind when I hear about leaders who are working so hard to be across the details of their team or business unit is being *stretched too thin*. I think of those leaders as being a bit like a rubber band, being stretched to its absolute limits. Everyone knows it's either going to snap or fly off and hit someone in the eye – even the rubber band knows this! And yet it continues to stretch and hold on, stretch and hold on. It is filled with tension and yet it's actually not being very productive.

The pace of work and the dynamic nature of organisational life means that things move and change quickly. Further, the sheer volume of work and information that flows through a relatively small team in an average organisation means that leaders have to be mindful of what they aim for – in terms of being up-to-date, involved in or directly managing the output of those they work with. This presents another obstacle for leaders who are ultimately trying to control how work is done and the outcomes that are produced. That's hard to do when things are changing fast. Overdoing by seeking control is not only inefficient for you, it also hampers the learning and productivity of others who are juggling many balls in the air. It results in frustration for all involved.

At the beginning of this chapter I introduced Lauren. She was constantly reworking her team members' output in an effort to prevent any criticism from her boss – trying to ensure that her team's work didn't make her look bad. In doing so, she knew deep down she was being inefficient and was causing real problems for her team members. They were not empowered to do their jobs, started to doubt their own competence and were missing opportunities for valuable feedback and learning so that they could gradually improve over time. Lauren was missing the biggest part of her role: to develop and coach others to facilitate their growth and help them become more high-performing.

The small voice in your head might be insisting right now: 'As a leader, I'm expected to be across what's happening in my team and the business. Isn't it okay to achieve and want high standards?' Well, it's always a matter of degree, and it depends on what you see as success. So, how *do* you evaluate success in your role as a leader? Does success equate to ensuring there are zero mistakes, even if it takes you working 80-hour weeks and micromanaging your team to achieve that? Or does success equate to something different – for example, having a balance between your personal and professional hours and giving others opportunities for growth?

 UNLOCKED TIPS

Micromanaging is a well-acknowledged management style. It can also be a direct outcome of Overdoing. So, how do you loosen the reins of control? Here are my tips:

- Control the controllables. Focus your energy on situations and people that you can influence and don't become absorbed by situations that are ultimately outside of your control. For example, remember that you can control your own behaviour and performance but you can't directly control the behaviour of those in your team when they represent you. You can *influence* that behaviour by coaching them, giving them constructive feedback and providing them with opportunities to learn, but you can't control it. Focusing too much on issues outside of your control (for example, whether a certain function will deliver their part of a project, or whether an external situation will create problems for your work) will only absorb your energy and ultimately slow you down.

- Remind yourself of the value of delegating (it helps you to multiply what you can do, for a start!). Start small, and make a mental note when you see it go well. I use a simple acronym that can help you get started: *IMS*. Try planning out one task you could delegate using this checklist:

  - *Identify*: choose the right person for the task (matching for skills and interests where possible). Make sure they are clear on the expected outcomes, and then try to get out of their way!

  - *Monitor*: as required based on the person's capability and how high the stakes are with the task. Give as much latitude as possible, especially when it comes to *how* they complete the task – remembering there is often more than one 'right' way to do something! The main thing is that the outcome is achieved. Don't be over their shoulder every minute.

  - *Support and coach*: let the person know they can reach you if they need to, and be available. Resist jumping in with the answers and taking over at the first sign of any difficulty. Try a coaching question instead: 'What have you tried so far? What else could you consider? Who else could help you with this?'

- Keep a gentle watch out for your need for recognition and the usual threat response as you let go of control – which is the fear of the unknown. When you feel the all-too-familiar stress or frustration if things aren't going well, try to maintain perspective. What is the worst-case scenario? And remember your reasons for delegating in the first place – it's productive, it gives others a chance to grow and it frees your capacity for all the other work you want to focus on!

RETHINKING MISTAKES

Mistakes happen, and occasional failures do not define your value as a leader or even as a person. This trap – distinct from the other traps of Overdoing – is based on your negative perceptions of any mistakes or blunders on the job that you make, however big or small. You end up Overdoing in an effort to avoid making any other mistakes under any circumstances.

When you're a leader, a mistake can range from inconsequential to highly significant, and even catastrophic in some situations, by function of the responsibility you hold. However, for most of us, mistakes don't result in anything that drastic. Yet, I've often seen leaders Overdoing their leadership by working unsustainable hours, insisting on double-checking every detail and taking the safest option when faced with the opportunity to try something new and different – all in a concerted effort to avoid getting something 'wrong'.

Upon making a mistake of some kind, many leaders will ruminate and feel concern, finding it difficult to let go, move on and learn from the experience. In these situations, the thought of making a mistake equates to failing to live up to an expectation either held by the leader themselves or by others. This can result in feelings of embarrassment and inadequacy, and can also feel incredibly frustrating.

When you respond to making a mistake with thoughts of 'I'm not enough,' your threat response will be triggered. Unless you catch yourself and take that deep breath to reset your brain, the response could either:

- *send you packing in fear* – withdrawing from that new role you are offered, or avoiding similar tasks in future even if it will cost you in terms of your development and growth
- *push you into defensive mode* – attempting to argue or defend your position, even after you've been clearly proven wrong.

If you allow either potential or actual mistakes to loom too large in your mind, this can lead you to become risk averse in an attempt to avoid future missteps – even though this behaviour will constrain your opportunities to grow and learn.

According to 'Wrongologist' and journalist Kathryn Schulz in her 2011 TED Talk 'On Being Wrong', as humans we learn at an early age that being wrong is a bad thing and that we should avoid it at all costs. We're also taught, overtly or otherwise, that if you discover that you've made a mistake, you should try to keep that fact to yourself. In her book *Being Wrong: Adventures in the Margin of Error*, Schulz makes the case that we're wrong about what it means to be wrong. Her argument is that 'being wrong is quite far from being a sign of intellectual inferiority'; rather, it's 'a vital part of how we learn and change'. Not only is making mistakes unavoidable, but it's also key to helping us become better people and leaders. Mistakes allow us to grow.

ARE YOU BEING REALISTIC?

Clearly, no one wants leaders running loose and making all sorts of mistakes just so they can happily chalk it up to learning and growth! Sometimes leaders' mistakes do have serious consequences – for example, creating significant damage to organisational reputation. No one wants to be that leader. Nonetheless, part of embracing the notion that *leadership is being human* means we also need to accept that leadership is imperfect, and that mistakes will be inevitable. To think otherwise is setting ourselves an unachievable target. Smart leaders also use the collective around them to help prevent mistakes, which is more robust than relying on themselves as a central point of focus. Even pilots have co-pilots to keep an eye out when flying a plane. No one should go it alone.

 UNLOCKED TIPS

Here's how to rethink the important role of making mistakes when it comes to your own learning and growth, along with that of your team and your organisation:

- From avoiding them at all costs, identify and work within the tolerable margin of error that you're able to embrace within the context of your role, project or task.
- Always frame mistakes that do occur as valuable opportunities to learn and continuously improve.
- Remind yourself that by facing up to and even sharing stories of times when you've gotten it wrong, you're

building trust with others as a function of your honesty. Mostly we assume that owning up will have the opposite effect and erode our status in others' eyes – this is not the case!

- Share the work of risk management across your team. Use the collective around you to help you anticipate issues, identify potential hurdles, come up with better solutions and be on guard to help mitigate those risks on your collective behalf.

It might be hard to embrace mistakes if you have a mental model of leadership that says leaders have to get it right. Also, if you're working in an environment of low psychological safety, it will feel much harder to own up to errors without feeling like they might be held against you. To address this, the best thing to do is to reset the way you see your role: from a sole figure in charge who can't stuff up, to a person working with a collective of others, achieving together and learning along the way. Think of yourself as a person who strives to do well but recognises that occasional missteps are part of the process of work and learning. By owning those mistakes when they do happen, you will always earn greater respect in the eyes of those you lead, in contrast to avoiding accountability or allowing those mistakes to mentally hold you back.

KNOWING WHAT COUNTS

Wisdom lies in understanding the difference between perfectionism and achievement. You can remain conscious of the need to meet others' expectations while becoming what I like to call a 'reformed perfectionist'. The key to doing this well is adjusting your own expectations to something that's achievable (maybe lowering the bar just a smidge, akin to the classic 80/20 rule!). At the same time, remember you still need to meet the expectations of your stakeholders – including those you report to, your peers, your team members and your customers. As I described in Chapter One, leadership only exists in the interaction between people. When one person views the other as a leader, that perception carries a set of expectations about what you do and how you operate. As such, you will always need to be conscious of those expectations and how you should factor them into your measures of success.

Wisdom lies in understanding the difference between perfectionism and achievement.

You can avoid Overdoing by ensuring you *know what counts*. This means rethinking the expectations you place on yourself as a leader. The term 'perfectionist' is defined by psychologists (Flett and Hewett) as a 'personality trait that is characterised by striving for flawlessness and having exceptionally high standards for performance, combined with tendencies to evaluate one's own or others' behaviour in an overly critical manner'. In other words, it's setting a *really* high bar and being relatively harsh in your appraisal of performance.

As these researchers have shown, perfectionism can either be *self* directed – for example, having really high expectations of yourself – or *other* directed, which is having high expectations of others. Perfectionism can also be what they describe as 'socially prescribed', where you assume that others (your peers, your boss, your friends, your family) have equally high expectations of you, often resulting in distress when you feel like you're not meeting those standards.

The strain that you bring on yourself and others by holding some of these perfectionist tendencies is potentially damaging. I've seen it affect people's health, wellbeing, job satisfaction and productivity. By overcoming this pattern, you'll be better able to find contentment in your work, feel a sense of pride and sustain your work efforts over time. Remember that perfect is impossible, at least for us mere mortals. Think about it – even engineers aim for excellence 'within tolerable standards', with caveats such as weight limits on bridges, assuming regular maintenance, allowing for environmental conditions and so on.

What are the tolerable standards for you, if not perfection? Dr Jen Douglas is a clinical psychologist from Stanford University who specialises in helping people understand and overcome perfectionistic tendencies. She points out that what looks perfect to you today will not necessarily be perfect in the future. Notions of perfection change and adjust according to our self-expectations and the situations we are in. Consider for example how someone who is Overdoing would have already-high expectations of themselves under one manager, and how these might significantly increase under a less supportive and more demanding manager in future. It's another reason why perfection is ultimately unattainable: our ideals and expectations keep shifting.

You might be thinking that high standards are exactly what we need in the world. Or maybe your concern is that others really *do* have these unrealistic expectations of you. What do you do then? If you have this swirling in your mind, remember the distinction between perfection and achievement. Achievement is realistic; it's stretching without negatively impacting yourself or others so much that the costs clearly outweigh the benefits. As Adam Grant is quoted as saying: 'Success depends on high standards, not being flawless. The target is not perfection – it's excellence.'

🔒 UNLOCKED TIPS

Here are some tips to help you deal with perfectionism:

- Learn to spot your perfectionism when it pops up. It can look different for different people. A perfectionism 'checklist' might include things like working longer hours, ignoring your own needs, feeling shame or like you're not enough, experiencing burnout or feeling a lack of satisfaction in your work (because it's never good enough). Being aware is the first step.

- Remind yourself regularly that there is often more than one 'right' way to do something. Your specific way of completing a task or producing a piece of work is not the only way to achieve the end result you and others are after. This thinking will significantly free up yourself and others to take different approaches and bring in fresh methods and ideas.

- Redefine your measures of success with consideration of your intrinsic motivators – your values, what really counts – combined with a realistic appraisal of the expectations others have of you. If you haven't done so in a while, check in with your stakeholders regarding their expectations so that you can keep these firmly in mind while re-evaluating what counts. A good way to define your own metrics of success is to answer these questions:
    - 'I will feel good about the impact I have as a leader when ...'
    - 'In six months' time, success in my role will look like ...'

> Once you've answered these for yourself, check that you and your trusted colleagues believe that those answers are achievable!
>
> - Honour your own needs – whether that's committing to and prioritising more rest, asking others for help, reducing the number of achievements you're aiming for or expanding the length of time to achieve them. These acts are not about letting yourself off the hook, they are to set you up for success.

Habits from the past and your current ways of operating might at first impede you from moving from Overdoing to knowing what counts. For example, having periods of time devoted to rest rather than constantly 'doing' can feel very uncomfortable for leaders who have been caught up in Overdoing. It won't happen immediately but practise makes (imperfect) perfection!

MOVING BEYOND

This chapter makes the case that leadership success is more to do with achieving through others, learning as you go and being clear on what counts, rather than being the 'hero' who never makes a mistake and strives for unrealistic standards.

The key here is to stop burning yourself out and causing unnecessary angst by Overdoing – whether that's trying to solve everything, being across everything, focusing on things beyond your control or avoiding situations where you might make a mistake or feel like you're out of your depth. Your aim is to start slowly letting go of control, while resetting your measures of success and focusing on what counts.

This chapter rounds out the three patterns of internal barriers for leaders in this book – Going Fast, Holding Back and Overdoing. Through holding up these mirrors and reading through the unlocked tips, I hope you feel more aware, motivated and ready to apply the practical approaches I've offered so you can overcome these barriers. In our final chapter, I focus on how to sustain those efforts, to help you stay unlocked.

CHAPTER EIGHT

Staying Unlocked

The last three chapters have all been dedicated to helping you think about your leadership in a new light. To reflect on how you want to lead, and become aware of the barriers that are getting in your way – leaving you feeling charged and ready to apply the practical tips I've shared along the way. Usually at this point, I hear leaders say 'I completely get this about myself. I'm ready to start. But … how do I make it stick?' This is the chapter where I give you the tools for staying unlocked.

Let's face it, we're all strapped for time and energy. You're expending effort trying to grow and develop as a leader, reflecting on your thoughts and behaviours and learning new ways of leading. If none of that development sticks over time, you're not going to get a good return on your investment! Your behaviour-change efforts won't create the positive difference you hope for. In other words, you will miss the opportunities that come from being unlocked – feeling greater job satisfaction, having a positive impact on those around you, achieving great outcomes at work and becoming an even more uniquely brilliant leader.

IT WON'T HAPPEN OVERNIGHT ...

Sustained change and growth are possible, and the rewards are great. *Sustained change* is continuing to evolve the way you behave as a leader, so that it sticks. *Growth* is about growing your capacity to see yourself and the world around you in a more expanded way than what you have in the past; basically, growing how you think. Both sustained change and growth are key to staying unlocked – keeping those barriers out of your way from leading in the way you want to lead.

There's a big difference between real growth and, say, attending training. When you attend training, you might listen to an expert talk about what you should do in a given situation. Even though you might nod along in agreement and take notes dutifully, attending some training doesn't guarantee that you'll go out and *do* anything differently with that information. In contrast, real growth means that you have internalised the idea that operating in a different way is valuable, that it's going to have benefits to you and is important to you. But it also means you go and put what you've learned into practice and continue to do so consistently over time. All of this is possible with awareness, support and self-compassion, and I will explain all of these steps as we go through this chapter.

MAKING YOUR INVESTMENT COUNT

Consider the estimated US$50-plus billion a year spent globally on leadership development training. A classic McKinsey research article made the case that many of these development dollars fail to make the intended difference – to create sustained behaviour change and improved leadership capability. McKinsey's research suggests that, among other things, most programs don't ensure leaders put their learning into practice in the real world. It also argues that programs often fail to address the root causes of behaviour – the underlying mindsets, beliefs or assumptions of that person. In other words, they don't get below the surface of the iceberg!

This latter point is supported by the 'immunity to change' concept developed by Dr Lisa Lahey and Dr Robert Kegan from the Harvard Graduate School of Education. Their research highlights that even when we *want* to change and see the benefits in doing so, our initial attempts just don't stick. Why? Because, Lahey and Kegan argue, there are often competing priorities deep within us, of which we may not even be aware. For example, consider an executive who genuinely wants to get better at empowering his team with greater decision-making power. The executive clearly sees the potential benefits, such as freeing up his own capacity and giving greater autonomy and job satisfaction to his team members. Yet despite this, change doesn't happen. Only after a lot of deep prompting and reflection, the executive finally starts to unpack what is really holding him back from making this shift: an assumption that if he gave up control, he would somehow become less valuable in the organisation. Once he understood the root cause of the issue – a hidden assumption that created a threat response – he was in a position to challenge that assumption, freeing him up to make the desired behaviour shifts.

LEARNING HOW TO LEARN

Beyond all the statistics and research on how to change human behaviour, let's take a moment to make it personal. Have a think about the last time you started a commitment you felt strongly about – maybe a new exercise regime, eliminating your plastics usage or cutting way back on your digital consumption. Think about how invested you were at the time and your reasons for wanting to make this change. Now think about the tension that inevitably started to come from slipping back into your old habits, despite your best intentions.

Let's face it, change can be hard. Learning how to behave and think differently is a skill in itself and not one that we're usually taught at school, university or even in most workplaces. We have to teach it to ourselves. Ideally, our leaders would teach us this skill over time – and maybe you, as a leader, can teach it to others in the future! As David B Peterson and Mary Dee Hicks wrote in their book *Development First*:

> **'Consistent reliable learning comes only with an understanding of how you learn.'**

Understanding how we learn allows us to continue to grow as leaders, and to adapt to all the changes that come as the world continues to evolve around us. Drawing on decades of research and practice from the fields of leadership, coaching and behaviour change, this chapter will show you how to overcome those barriers for good and stay unlocked.

REWIRING FOR GOOD

Growing as a leader is an ongoing commitment to the gradual rewiring of the brain. We all understand how the brain can change through neuroplasticity and rewiring our neural pathways through the creation of new habits. Put simply, rewiring doesn't mean doing something a bit differently for a short period, but embedding a different way of thinking (and therefore behaving) that is sustained over time. Rewiring for *good* means that these points of growth will hopefully have a hugely positive impact on you and those around you.

Real and sustained change can take longer than we sometimes imagine, so it's important to know it's not a race against others. In the pursuit of growth, remember that it is a long game – it's a marathon, not a sprint. And I hate to break it to you, but your growth isn't ever going to be 'finished and done', like a tick-the-box situation. It's a work in progress, and everyone is running their own marathon. Comparing yourself to others is redundant and unhelpful. Perhaps you're just starting out in the pursuit of growth and focusing on certain behaviours you want to change. If you go out and start comparing yourself to someone you see as advanced, who seems to have it all worked out, this could be inspiring – but it can also feel disheartening. It's pretty unfair and very unnecessary to compare yourself to the impression you have of someone else. Everyone is still growing, even those who appear to be much further along the path. Any day is a good day to start your development in earnest.

You will experience periods of growth at various times in your leadership and life. However, my observation is that growth is typically not a linear experience, but a gradual upward trajectory with accelerated parts followed by plateaus (and sometimes a slight sidestep!). At work, it might be something like a new job or a promotion that spurs a period of growth for some months. In your personal life, maybe it's going through other situations, such as becoming a new parent, moving countries or studying.

All of these situations that life might throw at you have implications for how you lead and how you learn. But then life settles a bit and perhaps you steady your development efforts for a while. That's natural.

GROWTH OUT OF THE COMFORT ZONE

One of the most accelerated periods of growth in my career was about seven years ago, when I left financial services. As I mentioned earlier in the book, for many reasons I had experienced burnout and was in need of change. As I transitioned into a new phase of my career, there were a couple of things that supported a real period of growth for me. First, I returned to psychology – the field I was most passionate about, but also somewhere I felt safe during a time when I needed to rebuild my confidence. When I got back into that work, I felt reaffirmed that psychology was something I loved doing and was pretty good at! I also had a lot of supportive people around me – a mentor who I had previously worked closely with and some wonderful, encouraging colleagues who inspired me and were only out to see me succeed. Shifting fields also gave me an opportunity to try new things and put myself out of my comfort zone in a manageable and steady way. I started taking on more responsibilities, honing new skills, developing new client relationships and practising in a way that I had not done before.

The biggest catalyst for my development though was working with a coach. That coach held up a mirror to my own thinking during this period and helped me to more clearly understand what I found difficult in my prior roles. Through that reflection, I came to realise those barriers at the time had a lot to do with the Holding Back profile I describe in this book. I was feeling as though I wasn't good enough and that was creating anxiety for me on a regular basis, particularly whenever I was about to try something new or really put myself out there. I was also looking for validation from others instead of giving it to myself, which definitely wasn't helping with the anxiety.

That coaching helped to deepen my awareness, but it also helped me identify specific practices that would help me rewire my thinking. Over time, instead of thinking I wasn't good enough and experiencing the subsequent anxiety, I caught myself before I was in that pattern and started to tell myself a new narrative – one that was based on a commitment to try new things, that challenged my assumptions that I would fail and that encouraged me to accept feedback from others when they told me I was doing a good job.

I'll be real – it wasn't a quick fix. It took a bit more than just reading a book or listening to a podcast. I needed some external support, particularly from my coach, and it took time. It took patience and kindness to myself, because sometimes I did fall back into that pattern of thinking I wasn't good enough, and felt the familiar anxiety that followed. But slowly and steadily, over 12 to 18 months, I started to notice a discernible shift – a positive difference in my thinking, less need to 'catch myself', less anxiety – to the point where I *knew* I had grown as a person.

If you're still doubting that people – or you, specifically – can change for good, remember what is at stake if you do not grow. Remember what the benefits of growth are to you and others. It's not about being perfect and it's not about hitting 100 per cent of your goals right away. It's also not about forgetting who you are or trying to be someone you're not. Ultimately, it's about trying: trying to become the leader you want to be. Even two steps forward and one step back is still a net of one step forward! For motivation, keep coming back to what's at stake for you; consider the costs of not growing in contrast with the benefits of growing over time. For focus, my advice is to pick *one* behaviour or thought pattern to work on, as you'll have more success than if you try to tackle lots of growth areas at once. We'll get into this in the next section.

Lastly, I want you to consider a time when you have had success in making a change in your behaviour, no matter how small or large. Perhaps it was ending an unhealthy friendship or relationship. Perhaps you stopped smoking. Perhaps it was choosing not to engage in an argument with your irritating uncle at family events. If you struggle to think of an example, ask a friend or a family member for a positive change they've seen in you in recent years and take stock of that. Believe them and take it as an example of your potential to grow. If you can do it once, you can continue to do it.

PICKING YOUR PRIORITIES

Successful change comes from focusing on one or two things, not trying to do everything at once. Your priorities should reflect both what matters to you in your role as a leader and what matters to those you are leading. If you're not clear on the former, you need to revisit your goals and values. If you're not sure about the latter, your first task is to ask them. As you think about your priorities, it's also important to be as specific as possible as to what you're attempting to change or develop. You will get a much better return on your efforts by doing these two things, as it makes development achievable and you're not going to bite off more than you can chew.

When I moved back into the field of psychology after a period in financial services, I focused on changing the thought pattern that was creating a lot of anxiety for me. It was also preventing me from taking on new and challenging assignments because I was Holding Back, and playing it safe. That barrier was the one thing that was making the biggest dent in my leadership. If I didn't adjust it, I knew that I couldn't unlock my potential, either for my own benefit or for my clients.

I knew through my coaching conversations that if I focused on changing that one thought pattern, it would ease my anxiety and free me to grow in other ways. This is so important. I always ask my clients when we look at their development priorities, 'What needs to happen first for you?' People always seem to know when you ask them that question where they need to focus first to allow change. It's a bit like working out where to stop the bleeding or plug the holes! That was definitely the case with me, too.

But what happens if you're told to change aspects of yourself that you don't think are a problem, or worse – that you feel are a core part of who you are as a person? A common one that I hear, particularly for women, is being told you're too much or not enough of *something* (insert adjective based on typical gender stereotypes). If you're told you're too much or not enough of something – for example, 'driven', 'emotional', 'opinionated' – it's going to be hard not to take it personally! If you're willing to consider the nature of the feedback, I suggest asking for more clarity from the person who provided it. Ask them to be specific in giving you an example of what they see you do, how the behaviour could be different and why that's important. If you're not convinced, it can also be helpful to test with others to understand more than one person's perspective. Consider again: is there a benefit to addressing this feedback, or a risk if you don't address it? Just because you receive a feedback-based suggestion doesn't necessarily mean it's the right priority for you. It boils down to motivation – if you don't truly believe that there is a real issue that needs to be addressed, you're unlikely to do much about it (and fair enough, too).

In the breakout below I've listed some suggested development priorities that relate back to the three patterns we've talked about in this book. These are not exhaustive, but they're some suggested points for you. If you're stuck and you can't come up with your own priorities, read these and pick one that resonates, or the one that you think would make the biggest difference for your leadership right now.

SUGGESTED DEVELOPMENT PRIORITIES

Going Fast:
- Investing more time planning ahead every month
- Setting my intentions before each big meeting
- Being more present in my interactions with others
- Slowing down to ask thoughtful questions

Holding Back:
- Balancing information-gathering with decisiveness
- Speaking with courage
- Saying yes to opportunities even if I doubt my abilities
- Putting forward my perspective more often

Overdoing:
- Delegating more tasks to my team
- Managing the amount of rework I do/corrections I make
- Focus on what's important (remember the 80/20 rule!)
- Draw on the team more to help solve problems

A word of caution (and I mean this sincerely): don't automatically focus on your 'weakness' – the thing you think you're no good at. Focusing only on stuff that you feel is not good about you can lead to frustration and feeling flat. It is hard to stay motivated if you're trying to fix something about yourself, when you doubt you're ever going to improve. Focus on the thing that you *want* to work on and that you believe will add value to your performance and impact as a leader, or will help you get ready for your next career move – this is what's known as your 'growth edge'. You want to feel motivated, and that will happen when you know the benefits that will come from your growth efforts. Focus on areas that can help you close any gaps between what's needed now in your role and what you have in place already. Consider the next three to six months – what will make the biggest difference to help boost your leadership? You could also focus on investing in your future self as a leader. What are the behaviours or skills that you will need in the future, in your organisation or in your field as a leader? If you're not sure, who could you ask to find out?

PLANNING MAKES PERFECT

With your priorities in place, it's time to set the plan. This can involve a development-planning template that your organisation might have, or you could use the classic SMART goals – whatever works for you. But the key is to write it down. After you write down your development goal, consider the factors that will help define your plan:

- Timeframes (for what length of time will I focus on this area? For example, three to six months)

- Actions (what am I going to do exactly? For example, get some advice, observe someone who is strong in this area, read up on how it works, and so on)

- Support (who else needs to be involved? Who can give me feedback?)

- Risks (what might get in the way – within myself or externally?)

Remember that your development priorities are likely to change over time, as a result of taking on a new role, the team changing around you or as you grow and achieve some of your earlier goals. Just make sure that when you do the work to set these priorities, you stay the course for a while. Try not to chop and change too much around your priorities before you've given it a solid crack and started to see the benefits of your hard work.

APPLYING NEW PRACTICES

Once you've identified your priorities and set your commitment and intentions in place around those, the rubber needs to hit the road. It's time to actually do something differently. It takes know-how, real-world practice and reflection to ensure that you regularly apply new practices and assess how you're progressing towards your goals. This is the good stuff. Once a leader becomes aware or learns something about themselves that they want to shift, usually their next step is to do something about it. They want to know what and they want to know how. That's what we're focusing on here.

One of the biggest arguments against doing the real work of development is lack of time; 'How can I possibly have time to do this when I'm so busy?' Partly it's getting real with the alternative – if you don't grow, you'll be treading water or, at best, dog-paddling your way forward. Your potential stays locked. The other point, though, is that you need to learn smarter, not harder. It's about finding ways to learn as you work, and work as you learn. It's learning how to weave your ongoing development into your everyday life, not adding another 'to-do' item on your never-ending list that – let's face it – probably won't get done.

The number one way you can take action is by finding out what to do differently – the 'know-how' part. What is it that you're going to put into practice? What does it look like as a behaviour or as a different thought pattern? For me, it was to replace the thought that I would likely fail when I tried something new, and to start believing other people's positive feedback. For the executive wanting to empower his team, it was coming up with the strategies to do just that.

Whatever priority you've set, you will need to come up with a game plan of what exactly you're going to think or do differently. How do you know what that's going to look like? You can start with using the content in this book related to the pattern or the priority that you've honed in on. That could be anywhere in Chapters Five to Seven. You can also ask a mentor or someone who's particularly strong in that area for advice. Or, if you are feeling a bit shy, you can observe that person in action and learn indirectly from how they operate. Lastly, you can do your own research. You can read books on the topic, watch TED Talks, access articles and do courses to get ideas about what to do differently with regards to that development area.

Once you've got the know-how, you need to put it into place and give it a go. It's like learning to ride that new bike you've bought.

You've got the wheels. You've bought the helmet. Now you need to go and take it out for a spin.

Aim for daily practice. Be intentional and look at your day ahead. Identify a meeting or a task that you have on your schedule for that day that will give you an opportunity to practise this thought pattern or behaviour. If you find yourself being distracted or in reactive mode in that moment, take a breath and hit the pause button. Gently reset your intention and carry on as best you can in that moment.

To be successful you must make space for reflecting on the leader you want to be and how you want to lead, then regularly assess how you're progressing towards or acting in alignment with that intention. Leadership development expert and author of *The Mindful Leader*, Michael Bunting, provides great advice in his book for honing your mindfulness as a leader if you would like to explore this further. But as a simple technique, after each meeting or interaction, I suggest you do a two-minute review. Take two minutes to pause, take a breath and ask yourself, 'How did that go? What worked well? What didn't go as planned? How do I know? What will I do differently next time?'

To be successful you must make space for reflecting on the leader you want to be and how you want to lead.

From your two-minute review, you can extend to doing a daily or weekly recap with yourself. How did you go over the course of the week when you observed your patterns of behaviour? To your mind, what worked and what didn't? Periodically, it will be valuable to round out these self-reflections with feedback from those working with you. This can be either formally through a 360-degree feedback process or survey, or informally through conversation.

COURSE-CORRECT, DON'T THROW OUT THE MAP!

Discomfort is natural through the process of development, especially for anyone who experiences elements of Holding Back (trying to avoid risks) or Overdoing (fixating on getting things 'right'). Remember, few people have everything sorted – we're all working it out as we go along. The new practices you are trying are unlikely to have catastrophic consequences for you or others, so let's bring down the stakes a bit. Learning to become comfortable with being uncomfortable is a critical skill for this crazy world we're leading in. The best way to tackle that is to redefine your view of success, just like we talked about in Chapter Seven. Focus on what you are learning through this process, not on what you are getting 'right'. And above all, try to think about your efforts as slight-but-regular adjustments. I think of it as a steering wheel motion – you're heading down a windy road, and you're adjusting slightly to the right or the left as the situation requires. You're not throwing out the car and starting with a new one. You're navigating the road as it comes, making things work with the car you have.

USING YOUR NETWORK

Using a mix of people in your network to help you stay unlocked is one of the smartest things that you can do. You can use different people in your network to help you test priorities that you've selected, give feedback on how your new practice is going and provide you with support along the way. This stuff is hard enough without attempting to go it alone. We all need support from our network as we grow.

Organisational researchers Rob Cross and Robert Thomas are experts in understanding the benefits of networks for leaders. In an article published in *Harvard Business Review*, they described four types of people in our network that can help sustain our success as leaders – power, information, support and coach. Each of these roles brings distinct value to a leader's network in the following ways:

- *Power:* those who are well-connected, can make things happen for you or can advocate on your behalf.

- *Information:* those who have valuable expertise or experience, who can teach you, or have informal knowledge of how things work in an organisation.

- *Coach:* those who will give you honest feedback, provide a balanced perspective and want to see you grow and succeed.

- *Support:* those who will encourage you always and be your safe landing place. They're people you can be comfortable opening up to when you are finding things difficult.

Of course, you are always the key person responsible for your own development. You need to set the intention, work out your priorities, take initiative, commit to the action and do the reflection. All of these things will get you a long way in your development, but not the whole way and you can't go it fully alone. You need others to make sure that your efforts are hitting the mark, and to make sure that you stay on track by getting that feedback and support along the way.

UNLOCKED TIPS

Create a network map for yourself that will help you in your learning and growth over the coming months. Think of people in your current and recent network that you can put into the following three categories (some people will sit across multiple categories – these people are extra valuable to you!):

1. *Development*. These people will give you honest feedback and advice. For example, you can test what you are working on by saying to them, 'I'm working on this part of my leadership. Is this something you think would be of value?' They can also provide you with know-how. These might be mentors who have ideas about what you could do differently in a certain area or can give you feedback on how you're going with this new practice. They need to be able to observe you in action and give you regular, honest and constructive feedback.

2. *Accountability*. These people will be your get-on-with-it buddies. They'll check in on your progress and help you answer the question, 'Am I doing what I said I would do?' Let them know your intentions, try to connect with them weekly over a walk or a phone call, and let them give you a hard time if you have been slipping back from your intentions a bit!

3. *Encouragement*. These people will be your cheer squad. These are the people who believe in you and your potential. When you doubt yourself, start to misstep or lose momentum, they will be the people who listen with empathy and remind you that you can do it.

Across all categories, consider people in your current network and people you've worked with or had in your world over the last couple of years. These people could be a former manager, a peer, members of your team, a client, a friend, or someone you used to work with as a trusted mentor. Think broadly and don't be afraid to reach out to reconnect or ask for their support. Most people love to be asked for advice and to be given the opportunity to help someone out – it's a natural response for many of us.

You might feel you don't know enough people to cover the three categories. Maybe you've been a little bit isolated over the last couple of years, and that's completely okay. Start with one person who you can informally chat to about the development that you're working on. It's far better than trying to go it alone.

PRACTISING SELF-COMPASSION

Self-compassion is something that I emphasise with all of my clients. It is so important in this fast-paced, high-standards world we're living in, with mental health and wellbeing as challenging as it's ever been. As you know, being a leader can be a lonely and tough job sometimes. So you have to show yourself a bit of kindness along the way.

There are lots of ways that you can practise self-compassion. At its core, it's about valuing the fact that you have unique and genuine strengths, and that you're willing to step up and take a leadership role. That in itself is something to hold in high regard. You are worthy as you are, and you deserve to give yourself kindness rather than beat yourself up. At the end of the day, leadership is so important and it's a great responsibility. But you are also a human being, and we're all deserving of humanity and grace.

Dr Kristin Neff is an associate professor in human development and regarded as the world leader on the topic of self-compassion. In her book *Self-Compassion* she describes the core components of self-compassion as showing self-kindness, understanding our common humanity and practising mindfulness. Neff writes: 'Self-appreciation and self-compassion are really two sides of the same coin ... one celebrates our strengths as humans and the other accepts our weaknesses. What really matters is that our hearts and minds are open.' She reminds us that we don't need to be perfect to feel good about ourselves or even to feel content. When you feel you can't change, that it's too hard or that other forces are too strong, have compassion for that feeling and start from there.

Neff's hopeful and encouraging words tell us that each new moment presents an opportunity for a different way of being. We can embrace both the joy and sorrow of being human, and by doing so we can transform our lives. It's a flashback to that shampoo ad in the 90s when model Rachel Hunter would assure us, 'It won't happen overnight ... but it will happen.' We just have to be kind to ourselves along the way.

When the tough taskmaster within you starts saying 'I won't get far if I'm too kind to myself' – just remember it's a balancing act. Development as a leader requires commitment and discipline to take action, without tipping too far into being hyper-critical of yourself so that you then lose momentum and set yourself up for failure. Keep maintaining a growth mindset and reminding your-self that you (and all of us) are works in progress.

If you're setting out to try a new behaviour or practice, maybe lower your standards a smidge, for a short time. Remember that you're learning here, so you're not going to know everything that you're putting into practice right away. Notice if or when you miss the mark in your new practice. Take that learning but don't dwell on it. You can start again tomorrow. Practise ultimate self-regard. You responded to the call to action at the beginning of this book and you aspire to unlock your potential as a leader. All of that carries inherent value. Your noisy, critical self-talk can be hard to overcome when it's been there for a long time. Keep going back to your support network as you need to. Your growth as a leader isn't going to happen overnight but you can make significant strides with a decent helping of self-compassion and the right people around you.

STAYING UNLOCKED

It takes conscious effort, but sustained change is possible, necessary and deeply valuable as you continue to grow as a leader. It's also a source of great reward and will give you huge opportunities throughout your career. From today, I hope you will let go of any assumptions that you can't meaningfully grow, because you absolutely can. I want you to try new behaviours and leadership practices – even if you hugely muck it up the first time – because it will be worth the effort in the long run. Most of all, I hope you reach out to the people who can help you along the way towards staying unlocked.

Imagine

It seems like an oxymoron: your unique leadership is needed in the world; but you are not the only one who experiences the internal barriers we have unpacked in this book. You are not alone – we all have our battles. Yet it is possible to overcome your internal barriers and grow in order to thrive and achieve your potential as a leader. Doing so will also place you in the best possible position to tackle the external barriers that we will all continue to face in an uncertain future.

I want you to imagine yourself 12 months from now. I want you to see yourself and your leadership clearly and truthfully after you follow the guidance I've offered in this book. I want you to recognise the true and wonderful things about who you are and how you lead others.

Imagine experiencing the lightness of showing up in your role every day and being comfortable to meet the challenges you will continue to face – meeting them head-on in a grounded place of knowing that you have it within you to try. You may not have all the answers, but you have all the heart. You can and will face those challenges by working with and through the collective effort of those around you. Imagine catching yourself when you misstep or fall back into a habit you swore you would overcome. When that happens, breathe and give yourself the kindness I know you would extend to a friend or colleague.

Imagine waking up in the morning, getting ready for work, reading your emails, taking phone calls and attending meetings – all while being centred with less stress, doubt and frustration than you experience now. You understand and accept all parts of yourself and the causes of those feelings, and you have a quiet and steady plan in place. You have practical strategies for shaping your own leadership.

Imagine being asked to speak about your leadership, or applying for a new role and answering the questions, 'Who are you as a leader? What do you bring to the table? How do you do that?' Imagine being able to quietly but resolutely articulate the answers to those questions in a way that feels authentic, as well as making you feel proud.

Imagine the sense of freedom, empowerment and honesty that you feel deep down because you understand who you are and because you're clear on your intentions. You know that you won't and can't get it right all the time, but hell, you're willing to give this work of leading others a red-hot crack.

Imagine the results that you'll deliver, the goals you'll achieve and the positive changes you'll influence, even if they only start with a ripple.

Imagine your customers and clients, your team and your peers, seeing you show up less stressed, noticing your quiet confidence and open-heartedness as you navigate all of what you face.

At this point down the road, imagine what else might be possible for you. What other impact could you have in the world? Consider the deeper potential you hold within you.

I imagined all of this for you when I set out writing this book. I want you to imagine this for yourself, too, so that you find a commitment to act on the insights that you have hopefully taken from reading this.

FINAL WORDS OF ENCOURAGEMENT

I know you want to have a positive impact and use your strengths when working with others to achieve great outcomes. This is the full essence of leadership. I know you want that because you wouldn't have been drawn to this book without really wanting those things for yourself. To achieve that, you need to believe in your own potential as a leader. Your logical brain can work out how to do the things in this book, but it is your *emotional* brain that will take you all the way when you're knocked down, confused, tired or forgot what you set out to achieve.

Start small with setting that first intention for your leadership. Make it a daily reminder and ask for help from someone you trust. Tell them what you're working on, then talk about it again after you've tried something new. Remember that change – even when it is something we genuinely want for ourselves and rationally understand to be a good idea – also brings discomfort because it means doing something that isn't yet natural to us. It might bring uncertainty about what it will mean for you and how people will see you. Generally, as humans, we avoid uncertainty and putting ourselves at risk. We go for the path of least resistance when it comes to our behaviour. So continue to go back to your why, what's at stake, the benefit of growth and the risk of not growing.

No single person can or should go it alone when it comes to leadership. I will be a champion for you and your leadership, and so will those around you once you are clear on the impact you want to have and how you want to help them achieve success too. I welcome you to this growing community of people I work with, who are committed to sharing their leadership with the world despite moments of doubt or occasional struggle. Those moments are part of the process of growth, and your impact as a leader will always be worth that effort.

My hope is that you unlock your potential as a leader; that you move forward believing that you are truly capable; and that your impact is felt in the most positive and powerful way that you intend.

References

Chapter One

Rebecca Cassells & Alan Duncan 2020, 'Gender Equity Insights 2020: Delivering the Business Outcomes', Workplace Gender Equality Agency, wgea.gov.au/newsroom/more-women-at-the-top-proves-better-for-business.

Chapter Two

Stephen R Covey 2004, *The 7 Habits of Highly Effective People: Powerful Lessons in Personal Change*, Free Press.

Norman Doidge 2007, *The Brain That Changes Itself: Stories of Personal Triumph from the Frontiers of Brain Science*, Penguin Life.

Carol Dweck 2007, *Mindset: The New Psychology of Success*, Ballantine Books.

David Kolb 1984, *Experiential learning: experience as the source of learning and development*, Prentice Hall.

McKinsey & Company 2021, 'Women in the Workplace 2021', mckinsey.com/featured-insights/diversity-and-inclusion/women-in-the-workplace.

Chapter Three

Edward de Bono 1999, *Six Thinking Hats: An Essential Approach to Business Management*, Back Bay Books.

Adam Grant 2021, *Think Again: The Power of Knowing What You Don't Know*, Viking.

Chapter Four

Max Bazerman 2015, *The Power of Noticing: What the Best Leaders See*, Simon & Schuster.

David B Peterson & Mary Dee Hicks 1995, *Development First: Strategies for Self-Development*, Korn Ferry Leadership Consulting.

Chapter Five

Daniel Pink 2011, *Drive: The Surprising Truth About What Motivates Us*, Penguin Putnam Inc.

Edward Deci & Richard Ryan 1985, *Intrinsic motivation and self-determination in human behavior*, Plenum.

Chapter Six

Adam Grant 2014, *Give and Take: Why Helping Others Drives Our Success*, Penguin Books.

Ethan Burris, Elizabeth McCune & Dawn Klinghoffer 2020, 'When Employees Speak Up, Companies Win', MIT Sloan Management Review, sloanreview.mit.edu/article/when-employees-speak-up-companies-win.

Chapter Seven

Richard Wilson 2013, *Anti Hero: The Hidden Revolution in Leadership & Change*, Osca Agency Ltd.

Ronald A Heifetz, Marty Linsky & Alexander Grashow 2009, *The Practice of Adaptive Leadership: Tools and Tactics for Changing Your Organization and the World*, Harvard Business Review Press.

Edgar Schein 2013, *Humble Inquiry: The Gentle Art of Asking Instead of Telling*, Berrett-Koehler Publishers.

Kathryn Schulz 2011, 'On being wrong', TED, youtube.com/watch?v=QleRgTBMX88.

Kathryn Schulz 2011, *Being Wrong: Adventures in the Margin of Error*, Ecco.

GL Flett & PL Hewitt 2002, *Perfectionism: Theory, research, and treatment*, American Psychological Association.

Jennifer Douglas 2022, drjenniferdouglas.com.

Chapter Eight

Mike Prokopeak 2018, 'Follow the Leader(ship) Spending', Chief Learning Officer, chieflearningofficer.com/2018/03/21/follow-the-leadership-spending.

Pierre Gurdjian, Thomas Halbeisen & Kevin Lane 2014, 'Why leadership-development programs fail', McKinsey, mckinsey.com/featured-insights/leadership/why-leadership-development-programs-fail.

Robert Kegan & Lisa Laskow Lahey 2009, *Immunity to Change: How to Overcome It and Unlock the Potential in Yourself and Your Organization*, Harvard Business Review Press.

David B Peterson & Mary Dee Hicks 1995, *Development First: Strategies for Self-Development*, Korn Ferry Leadership Consulting.

Michael Bunting 2016, *The Mindful Leader: 7 Practices for Transforming Your Leadership, Your Organisation and Your Life,* Wiley.

Rob Cross & Robert J Thomas 2011, 'Managing Yourself: A Smarter Way to Network', Harvard Business Review, hbr.org/2011/07/managing-yourself-a-smarter-way-to-network.

Dr Kristin Neff 2015, *Self-Compassion: The Proven Power of Being Kind to Yourself,* William Morrow Paperbacks.

About the Author

Rearn Norman is a psychologist and leadership coach who became fascinated with 'what makes us tick' at a weirdly young age.

She now works as a facilitator, keynote speaker and executive coach with senior leaders and their leadership teams. Her practice is based on almost 20 years of consulting and industry experience working with ASX-listed, private and public sector organisations across Australia in the fields of psychology, leadership and organisation development.

Rearn's home base is Melbourne, Australia, where she lives with her husband and two young sons. She spends an inordinate amount of time standing beside footy fields (usually in the rain), and a lot less time attempting to do yoga and go for the occasional run.

You can get in touch or find out more by visiting her website at **rearnnorman.com.au** or connecting on LinkedIn.

Acknowledgements

Three years before I wrote *Unlocked*, I was speaking at a conference when someone in the audience came up and told me I should write a book. I awkwardly laughed at the time, but it hit a nerve because deep down I knew it was what I most wanted to do.

It took me two and a half years to build the courage to start, which possibly would never have happened at all were it not for the encouragement I received from some of my dearest family, friends, colleagues and clients who saw the potential in this book even before I did.

My heartfelt thanks:

- To Kath Walters, the best book coach anyone could possibly ask for. Thank you for your expertise, creativity, patience and humour! You have made me obsessed with finishing the things I start, for which I thank you greatly.

- To Michael Hanrahan and Brooke Lyons, for the publishing and editing brilliance that took my (at times incoherent) words and turned them into what you see here. Your passion for books and encouragement for *Unlocked* was everything that got me over the line.

- To my earliest readers who made the time and effort to read my early manuscript and help me sharpen it into focus – Jamila Rizvi, Dr Marcele De Sanctis, Lisa Birch and Jack Ngo. Your suggestions were as appreciated as your belief in the value of this book, and I'm so grateful for both.

- To Joei, who started the whole journey. For connecting me with my coach, for sharing your many gifts with the world and encouraging me to find and share mine.

- To my family – Mum and Dad, Lauree and Stuart – without you I would not be the person I am. Thank you for always supporting me and connecting me to what matters.

- To Maddie, Xander and Campbell – I hope you all continue to unlock the truly deep potential that lies in each of you. I'm honoured to watch you all grow and can't wait to see the impact I know you will have in the world.

- And, to Philip – for keeping me company during the many late nights as I wrote this book, and for always believing in me, especially in the times I never seem to be able to.

- Lastly – to all the leaders I have had the privilege to work with over the years; thank you for inspiring me to write, and for all the hard work that you do. This book is for you.